INDIA

INDIA

MARTIN HÜRLIMANN

with 352 photographs
27 in colour

THAMES AND HUDSON · LONDON

Translated from the German by D. J. S. Thomson

THE VERY NAME 'India' has associations for us which no other country in the world can evoke. Europe first became aware of the fairy-tale world it conjures up when travellers returned with tales of the Grand Mogul and the Maharajas and of the fabulous splendour of their courts. The sense of awe inspired by such worldly magnificence was soon followed by admiration for the wisdom and elegance of Sanskrit literature and for the contribution it had made to world culture as one of the oldest members of the Indo-Germanic groups of languages. Then came the first pictures, rich in motifs for the most lavish operatic scenarios: palm-groves, marble columns and temples with strange figures, gods with many arms or with heads of animals, monsters that symbolize the deepest instincts of emotional and spiritual life. And as this ancient world emerged from obscurity, the pall of dust that lay over it also became visible, the dust of the long drought, which settles upon roads and fields and villages, the dust in which lean and hungry people live and work, wander and pray.

Today the name 'India' no longer merely conjures up vague images of a strange and distant land; we have seen the apostles of non-violence taking to the sword, and we have heard the twin voices of national pride and personal humility; extremes of materialism clash with extremes of idealism, the urge to contemplation and self-abnegation with the urge to action, the backward pull of age-old traditions with a desire to move forward. Political, economic and social problems are mounting alarmingly and continue to mount even as attempts are made to solve them. A rapidly increasing population—three hundred, four hundred, five hundred million—is trying to discover what role it can play in the twentieth century and in the great family of nations. For India is in the throes of a revolution which goes to the very roots of her being. Despite her great antiquity as a people, despite the fact that she had already developed a culture and way of life of her own thousands of years ago, she finds herself today confronted by a world which no longer permits isolationism. A people that once lived outside time is fighting to gain its historical identity.

Let us look first at India as a purely geographical concept. In general it covers the territory bounded in the north by a gigantic range of mountains which separate it from the rest of Asia, the three great rivers Indus, Ganges and Brahmaputra and the triangle of the Deccan which stretches southwards to the Indian Ocean and into the tropical zone.

The Indian sub-continent is one of the oldest in the world and has undoubtedly undergone considerable geological changes throughout the ages. The Deccan, the oldest landmass in

India, is for the most part a vast high plateau. The Western Ghats, which drop steeply into the Arabian Sea, are covered with luxuriant tropical forests and inhabited by primitive tribes. To the east, on the other hand, the plateau slopes gradually and carries the great rivers of southern India from their sources near the Arabian Sea across almost the entire peninsula to the Bay of Bengal. To the north of the Deccan plateau the Vindhya mountain range has repeatedly acted as a brake on migrations from the densely populated valleys of the Indus and the Ganges and became a sort of natural boundary between the Indo-Aryan and, in the south, the Dravidian racial and language groups, although it did not succeed in halting the spread of the Hindu-Vedic religion or, at a later date, the expansionism of the Muslim princes.

On the Malabar coast, in the south-west, there is never any shortage of water. The coconut-palms reflected in the clear water of the canals give an illusion of natural fertility but on closer inspection one discovers that Kerala with its seething population, dependent on imported foodstuffs, has very real problems. On the eastern coast water-conservation plays a more important part, and there are still vast areas waiting to be turned over to the cultivation of rice; on the top of the Deccan plateau, however, drought is an almost insoluble problem. Masses of eroded primeval rock project like great islands from the surrounding plain, as for example in the rock-temple of Tiruchirapalli, at Sravanbelgola, Vijayanagar and Bundelkhand. At Mahabalipuram the 'rathas' and caves with their reliefs were hollowed out of these rocks. At Vijayanagar and Golconda the old crystalline rock-layer has produced a jumble of enormous boulders which look as if they have been thrown down by Cyclops.

Farther north, in the Aravalli range, in the mountain fastnesses of the Rajputs, on Mount Abu, the fold in the rock, which goes back to one of the earliest stages in the earth's geological transformation, has been preserved in long mountain-ridges. It is from this area, from Jodhpur, Ajmer and Jaipur that the famous white marble of the Taj Mahal and the Moguls' palaces comes. Somewhat later than the original rock-formation of the Deccan but still in the early stages of the earth's geological history the horizontal Purana layers emerged, evidence of which can be seen, for example, in the mountain-fortress of Gwalior and at Sanchi, where erosion has caused the whole landscape around them to sink. Their yellow and red sandstone is excellent building material and was employed in most of the palaces and tombs in Delhi, Agra and Fatehpur Sikri.

In the medieval stage of the earth's history, in the middle of the cretaceous period, there were volcanic eruptions in the north and north-west of the peninsula, which threw up huge masses of basalt (the Deccan trap). The step-formations which resulted are particularly common in the area east of Bombay, where they can be clearly recognized from the plane as it flies in from Aurangabad. At times a solitary mountain is all that remains. A striking example is Satrunjaya, surmounted by its Jain temples, on the Kathiawar peninsula. Thanks to the durability of basalt, the caves of Ellora, those gigantic sculptures in stone, have remained in a remarkable state of preservation.

The northern barrier of the Himalayas, the highest mountain-range in the world, did not emerge from the sea which bounded India's primeval landmass until more recent times, around the middle and end of the Upper Tertiary period. The lowest part of the range, the Siwalik Hills, is one of the most recent mountain-formations we know of. Alone among the Himalayan countries, Kashmir in the west, a place of great natural beauty, has always remained open to penetration and invasion from outside; Nepal, on the other hand, a long, mountainous country, managed to preserve a precarious independence between the Indian and Chinese empires, while the small principalities of Sikkim and Bhutan to the east have always looked to their powerful Indian neighbour for protection. Still farther to the east the mountains of Burma, covered in tropical forests, inhabited by primitive tribes and largely inaccessible—as recently as the Second World War they halted the Japanese invasion—separate India proper from the countries of Indochina.

The only breach in the subcontinent's strong natural defences is in the north-west, although even here there are outcrops of the high mountain-barrier. Time and again the rugged tribes-men from the north moved down into the fertile plains and the Indians were usually no match for the ferocity and superior strategy of the invaders or for their more efficient form of government. The most dangerous enemy the conquerors had to contend with was the climate; the torrid summer heat bred apathy and mutiny.

India's population is largely dependent on the great river-valleys of the Indus, Ganges and Brahmaputra. Their waters, rising in the Himalayas, threw up deposits which went to form the vast plain between the mountains. The Indus, which gave the country its name, flows into the Arabian Sea; its two sister-streams debouch together in the Bay of Bengal. The Ganges plain in particular and that of its most important tributary, the Jumna, stretching from Agra to the pilgrim-centres Allahabad and Benares, to the ancient imperial city Paliputra near modern

Patna and to the port of Calcutta, India's largest city, was the birth-place of much of India's finest culture; about half India's population lives in this area alone. One village with its fields follows closely on another, and it is here, in these countless village communities with their subsistence cultivation and a way of life which has changed little since the time of the Buddha, that India's focal point still lies, that the struggle against starvation, against lethargy, against an imposed or a self-engendered serfdom will be lost or won.

The rhythm of life is dictated by water. The greater part of the country is dry for more than half the year. When the heat becomes oppressive in spring and summer and the supplies of water become increasingly scarce, when the soil cracks and threatens to become desert and when even the great rivers almost disappear in their broad beds, India awaits the yearly miracle of the monsoon, which brings abundant, cooling showers of rain. Within a few days the grey wastes are covered with green, the rice fields are under water and man thanks his gods for their gifts.

The pattern of cultivation reflects this interchange of drought and rainy periods. Artificial lakes and ponds are scattered throughout the entire country; they are a feature of the temples as well as of the princely residences. It was one of the responsibilities of the 'semindar' or land-owner to ensure the survival of his land and of the peasants by seeing to it that the water reservoirs were properly maintained. And when roads and railways came to be built, it also fell to the modern state to construct and maintain canals and dams—the building of dams has become symbolic of the Republic's entire urgent development programme.

The rivers are sacred. The great pilgrimages take place on certain days at such holy bathing-places as Allahabad at the confluence of the Jumna and the Ganges, where hundreds of thousands, even millions, gather from all parts of India. Daily ablutions in a river or pool, particularly in the early morning, are for the Hindu a spiritual as well as a physical necessity. Ever since the time of the Vedas the ambition of every Brahmin villager has been a temple in which to pray, a river or pool in which to bathe, and, only third in priority, a house in which to live.

In the south every temple has its own pool. Most of the sacred rites involve washing. The dying are carried to the riverbank, to one of the sacred bathing-places, where, their feet dipped in the water, they can breathe their last. The dead are also carried to a funeral pyre on the river-

8

bank, where the next-of-kin sets the wooden pyre alight and in due course the ashes are borne away by the river.

The subcontinent which we know as 'India' and which evokes in our minds such a clear and precise geographical image is inhabited by peoples who are much more widely assorted than the nations of Europe. Three of the world's major racial groups are in India and have inter-mingled at various levels: dark Dravidian types in the north with a negroid admixture in some of the primitive forest tribes, yellow-skinned Mongols, and light-skinned Indo-Europeans who in their sacred scripts make frequent use of the term 'Aryan' which has been so misused in our century. ('Arya' means freeborn or noble.) The origins of the first inhabitants are lost in the mists of prehistory. From the great mass-migrations the Dravidians emerged as the dominant tribes with the predominant culture, before the Indo-Aryan migration from the north-west left its own stamp on the country as far as the Vindhya mountains and gave it its reputation as the Land of Holy Wise Men. Fourteen different languages and a great many dialects are spoken and written in some form or other. The Dravidian languages of the south, such as Tamil (Madras), Telugu (Andhra Pradesh), Malayalam (Kerala) and Kanarese or Kannada (Mysore), have less in common—apart from a few phrases from holy scripture—with the language most widely spoken in the north, Hindi, than Hindi has with German, a member of the Indo-Germanic group; like Bengali, Urdu, Marathi and Gujarati, they have a rich literature.

The political history of India presents a picture that is almost as confusing in its complexity. As British India covered the entire subcontinent, we have come to regard the two concepts of India, the historical and the geographical, as identical, but the more stable kingdoms usually only comprised at most a part of the country—about the size of one of the states in the German Federal Republic—and even the occasional, ephemeral empire is not to be compared with the sort of state with its highly developed army, administration and ideology which the Romans and the Chinese created. Although there were periods when the somewhat loose overlordship of one of the great rulers such as the Grand Mogul was recognized, until recent times the greater part of the country was divided up into countless principalities, some reasonably large, others extremely small, and republican communities in which the village was the centre of public life. But 'India', the vast area between the Himalayas and Adam's Bridge, which leads across to Ceylon, has long since become something more than a geographical concept, for, despite the fact that there are no spectacular achievements or personalities for the historian to seize upon, India has produced one of the great cultures known to man, which transcended the barriers of race, language and principalities and gave the nations their law.

The word 'Hinduism' is a collective term which conveys both the splendour and the burden of the great heritage which India has brought with her into the twentieth century, which has gone, in fact, to make up the modern state of India, excluding Pakistan, a predominantly Islamic country, and therefore excluding also the north-western Indus valley and, in the east, the mouth of the Brahmaputra between West Bengal and Assam. The Indian Republic, with which we are solely concerned in this book, is described in its constitution as a secular state, it guarantees religious freedom and has never felt entirely happy about the formation of an Islamic state in what was formerly Brahmavarta (Holy Land); but Hinduism, which is the religion of 85% of the population, has determined the country's social structure and spiritual values for over two thousand years, is the dominant theme of its literature and art, is worshipped in thousands of temples of all ages throughout the land and is glorified in millions of sculptures.

Ever since Sir John Marshall's excavations after the First World War we have known that, even before the Indo-Aryans appeared, there was a highly developed city culture in the Indus valley, traces of which can still be found as far as Rajasthan. Its decline in the second millenium BC coincides roughly with the appearance of the first Indo-Aryans; yet the two are not necessarily linked, unless one chooses to connect the name 'parumdara' (destroyer of cities), given to the god-king Indra, with the conquest of the last fortified towns in the Mohenjodaro civilization. The cities on the Indus are reminiscent of the early civilizations in Mesopotamia. Time and again when there is a new civilization, a fresh invasion or migration, the signs point to the north-west.

The Indo-Aryans are presumed to have come originally from Persia. They arrived in several successive waves. The *Rig Veda*, oldest of the Indo-Germanic texts, which consists of more than a thousand hymns handed down by the rishis (seers) from generation to generation, depicts the Indo-Aryans as a people of shepherds and warriors organized in family groups and village communities. Presumably they only acquired the arts of ploughing, pottery and weaving when they came in contact with the ancient Indus civilization. The sharp distinction between the fair complexion (varna) of the invaders and the darker-skinned, smaller natives they found in India and treated as slaves gave rise to the caste system. According to the *Rig Veda*, when the primeval man was sacrificed, from his head came the Brahmans, from his arms the Kshatriyas, from his loins the Vaisyas and from his feet the Sudras. Between the Brahmans, who as repositories of the divine message succeeded in establishing a dominant position that was never challenged, and the lowest of the castes, the Sudras, came the Kshatriyas who were warriors and princes, and the Vaisyas who were artisans and traders. In the course of time these four main castes broke up into subcastes, of which there were more than two thousand at the beginning of the present century. Although many Hindus will admit that they themselves do not know to which particular caste they belong, it is still true to say that those who did not succumb to the lure of the great cities founded by the British were almost inevitably caught up—and still are—in the closely woven net of ruthless caste laws. The Untouchable or 'harijan', like the Unbeliever, is denied access to the temple, no Brahman may offer him water and to a caste Hindu even the shadow of an Untouchable is unclean; but at least he is not obliged to fast or to observe any other religious rules.

The Vedas were followed by the Upanishads and other holy scripts, which reached a magnificent climax in the two great epics. The *Mahabharata* with its hundred thousand verses, which took a very long time to complete and extends right up to the Christian era, describes the war of the 'Bharata succession', which ended in a victory for the Pandavas over the Kauravas; it contains the famous philosophical poem *Bhagavad Gita*, in which the god Krishna explains the duties of a warrior to Arjuna. The *Ramayana* is attributed to one single poet named Valmiki and tells the story of Prince Rama's expedition to Lanka (Ceylon) to rescue his wife Sita, who had been carried off by the demon prince Ravana.

Some time after the birth of Christ the swelling tide of deism spread to India. The place of the old Vedic gods such as Brahma and Indra was taken by Vishnu, the Penetrator or Protector. He also reveals himself as Krishna and Rama, legendary figures based perhaps on actual princes during the Vedic period. Beside him, and no less powerful, stands Siva, an ascetic who has sat for thousands of years on Mount Kailasa, where the Ganges flows out of his hair, the god of dancing, destruction and death, whose fertility is symbolized by the lingam. The principal gods, their consorts and their acolytes take innumerable forms. Parvati, for example, Siva's lovely wife, is also the fearsome mother-goddess Kali Durga.

While one is made aware, throughout India, of the vital role played by religion, a role which led to the division of the country into two separate states as recently as the middle of this century, it is as well to realise that the word 'religion' does not have the same meaning here that we are accustomed to give it. Dominating all else is *Karma*, the doctrine that our actions have a continuing effect upon our lives and on our personal destiny, from which we cannot escape even in successive states of existence. But theism, pantheism, polytheism and atheism also have their place in this doctrine. The act of prostration, the ringing of bells and the offering of flowers may represent to one Hindu divine service in the true sense of the term, whereas another will see in the figures he worships—or so at least he will tell a stranger—the embodiment of eternal thoughts. And washing in holy water is purification in the fullest meaning of the word. As in every other country, the priests have contrived to canalize divine worship into specific ritual forms, but the sacred scriptures, in which religion and philosophy, history and folklore have been transformed into poetry, have remained free from any such regimentation. Here all else is subordinate to the image and symbol of a reality which far transcends all the precepts of human reason.

Like the poets, the temple-builders and the stonemasons parade before the eyes of earthly mortals a bewildering profusion of images representing a cosmos that stretches far beyond their known horizon. Within the strict iconographic confines laid down by tradition there was still room for variety in depicting the principal godheads and their attributes; they are frequently surrounded by hosts of other gods, demons, celestial dancers, human or animal attendants, or they become interchangeable with ancient local nature-gods. Siva becomes Vishnu and Vishnu Siva. Siva also appears in the dual form of Ardha-narisvara, half man, half woman. Brahma, the old Vedic god, has four heads, Siva's son Ganesha, a bearer of good fortune, has an elephant's head, and four or more arms are the rule rather than the exception. Here man is not the measure of all things, he is merely one of many forms in which the god manifests himself. The size of the figures varies in deliberate relation to the environment from a mere hand's breadth to the almost twelve feet high head of Siva in his threefold capacity of creator, preserver and destroyer in the cave of Elephanta.

It is this message, transcending all scriptural and racial differences, that has united India. For centuries, in fact for thousands of years pilgrims have been travelling through the ephemeral kingdoms of this world, from the tropics in the south to the snowfields of the Himalayas in the north where Siva sits enthroned, travelling from one shrine to another—and whenever possible

3 (OVERLEAF) WOMEN WATER-CARRIERS NEAR DELHI

2 SARNATH

4 VISHNU

5 SHIVA

visiting the seven which are particularly holy—and with endless patience they carry the brass container with the precious Ganges water from Benares twelve hundred miles to the temple of Rameswaram on Adam's Bridge, where, in the holiest of holies, the water helps to cool the lingam set up by Rama.

Time and again Hindu sects broke away and, in some cases, set up their own religious communities in an attempt to free themselves from the rigid caste system of the Brahmans. This is how Buddhism and Jainism arose in the sixth century BC. Their founders were both members of the Kshatriya caste; among their followers were many princes and, in the case of the Jains, merchants. Buddha's teaching, which appealed to all temperaments and all classes of society, spread rapidly through the Ganges valley to the Punjab, to Afghanistan and even south beyond the Vindhya mountains, and only about a thousand years later was there a revival of Hinduism which enabled the Brahman to regain the upper hand. The Jains also lost ground and with it the protection of powerful princes, but they have nevertheless survived to this day in India as a small yet active and highly disciplined community; their holy mountains covered with temples can be seen in all parts of the country as evidence not merely of their devoutness but also of their wealth. Their founder Vardhamana, known as Mahavira (great hero), is believed to be the last of twenty-four Tirthankaras (those who pave the way to salvation in Nirvana), and it is possible that the twenty-third Tirthankara, whose name was Parsvanatha, had an actual historical prototype in a well-known ascetic.

Although Buddhism has long since ceased to be practised as a religion in the country of its origin, no picture of India would be complete without it and it also made an immense contribution towards awakening India's national consciousness. The founder of a world religion, whose features became familiar to millions even as far away as Japan as the symbol of Asiatic spiritual power, Buddha has remained ever since the greatest Indian of all time, and although the historical personality is scarcely visible amidst the profusion of legends, there is still enough evidence to show that one outstanding man alone could by the sheer radiance of his personality achieve this effect. The first historical events which did not evaporate in poetic imagery centre around his life and teaching, and the capital of the Asoka pillar of Sarnath with the Wheel of Learning, which the Enlightened One set in motion with his first sermon, can be seen today on the Head of State's flag.

What little we know of the historical Buddha has had to be gleaned from the occasional references in the sacred scriptures which appeared after his death: sermons, conversations and parables, some in poetic form. Many of the traditional events described in them can be found in almost identical form in the stories of Vardhamana, the Mahavira of the Jains. In all probability the man whose name was Siddhartha or Gotama (also Gautama) was born around 624 BC, the son of a certain Shuddhodana and his wife Maya, both from the Shakya clan, at Kapilavastu in the Terai of Nepal near the present Indian border. He appears to have left home between the ages of twenty and thirty, abandoning his young wife and their firstborn, in order to lead the life of a wandering monk, like countless Indians before and after him. After years of penance and a vain search for truth, he found inner tranquillity at Gaya in what today is the state of Bihar. Having become a Buddha or Enlightened One, he made his way to Benares, meeting-place of pilgrims and wise men, where he proclaimed his new found knowledge and gathered scores of disciples around him. He continued well into old age to wander from place to place with his begging bowl, collecting thousands of followers. The 'four Aryan truths' proclaimed by him are handed down as *Dukkha*, knowledge of the suffering of everything born, *Samudaya*, knowledge of the origin of suffering, *Nirodha*, conquest of suffering, and *Magga*, the middle way, which leads to the conquest of suffering. To our minds, the prospect of Nirvana, the void which awaits those who are delivered from the cycle of rebirth, suggests a profound pessimism, but to his followers, on the contrary, it was the only way to overcome the inexorable causality of their existence. Before his Enlightenment he had come to realise the pointlessness of his previous life of penance and had achieved instead a balance of body and mind. The image of the Buddha as portrayed by his disciples has always been one of relaxed and cheerful kindliness, which marks him out from all other Indians, and with it a suggestion of aristocratic superiority.

About the middle of the third century BC Buddhism found its greatest champion in Asoka, the grandson of Chandragupta, founder of the Mauryan Empire. He is reputed to have summoned a Council, similar to the Council of Bishops which Constantine was to summon later at Nicaea, in order to reunite the successors of the religion's founder, who had started to break up into rival schools and follow divergent paths. The destinies of nations are all too often shrouded in obscurity, until some bloody battle throws them up in harsh relief—and the Ganges valley was no exception—but this pious emperor emerges from the past standing out head and shoulders above all other Indian rulers: the columns which were erected in various parts of his far-flung empire and which were lavishly inscribed provide the first concrete evidence of this great civilization and of one of its leading men. In erecting these memorial columns. Asoka made a unique contribution to Indian history; but these edicts in stone, which were clearly intended for future generations as well as for his own subjects, also show that he was a true son of India. He does not glorify his government's achievements; he is much more concerned to underline the transitory nature of all worldly fame and calls upon his peoples to follow him along the road prescribed by Buddha, which leads to knowledge and renunciation. At the same time he makes no attempt to establish Buddhism as a state religion. Non-believers are not persecuted, and it is worth noting that even after his time there were no religious wars in India. The references in the edicts to contemporary events also make them documents of inestimable value to the political historian. Thus the following passage, which is a remarkable testament for any ruler to make, is both reportage and personal confession:

Immediately after the Kalingas had been overthrown, His Sacred Majesty began to take the Dharma (doctrine) under his zealous protection, to submit himself to the Dharma and to issue the instructions embodied in the Dharma. In so doing His Sacred Majesty felt a growing sense of guilt that he had fought the Kalingas; for the subjection of a previously free people leads to massacre and captivity. This causes His Sacred Majesty profound grief and fills him with remorse . . . For His Sacred Majesty wishes all living creatures to enjoy security, freedom, peace of mind and happiness. And may this pious decree serve as a re-minder to our sons and grandsons that they should not regard it as their purpose in life to make fresh conquests, unless they are conquests to be achieved by patience, kindness and humility.

In the period after Asoka's reign, when Buddhism developed in two main forms, that of the Hinayana (Little Vehicle) and that of the Mahayana (Great Vehicle), and spread to other countries, and when at the same time Brahmanism was gaining a new lease of life, two Buddhist pilgrims from China gave an account of their travels which also includes a reliable report on conditions in India. Around AD 400 Fah-hsien set out on his adventurous journey through the deserts and mountains of Central Asia to the shores of the Indus and the Ganges, and two centuries later Hiuen-tsang wrote a no less fascinating and even more detailed account of his journey, in which he paints a dazzling picture of this politically mature country with its wealth of monasteries and places of pilgrimage, a country which, until fresh invaders, Mohammedans and Christians, arrived from the west, was utterly cut off from the rest of the world.

With the Muslim invasion in the eleventh century India's position underwent a radical change. Ever since the Indo-Aryans had entered the country from the north-west, the Indus valley had been the first goal of any migrants or invaders. The Persian emperor's troops crossed the mountains of Afghanistan and annexed the Punjab and Sind. And after Darius' empire had collapsed before Alexander's army, the great Macedonian set out on his famous march to India. The art of early Buddhism in particular was greatly influenced by Persian and Greek art; goods, and with them ideas, travelled not only from west to east but also from east to west. Alexander's successors came to an agreement with Chandragupta, the founder of the Mauryan Empire, and Seleucus Nicator sent Megasthenes to the court at Pataliputra. Unfortunately the memoirs of these ambassadors, like the reports of other Greeks, have only come down to us at second hand. At the beginning of the eighth century the full force of the Arab expansion was already making itself felt in India: provoked by pirates, the Muslims had moved up the Indus from the sea as far as the border of Kashmir and had occupied Sind. But it was not until 1001 with the conquest of Peshawar by Mahmud of Ghazni that the succession of campaigns from the mountains began, which were to establish the domination of Islam in India; in 1033 one of his generals reached Benares and his successors gained control of the Punjab. In 1176 Muhammad Ghori began his invasions, defeated the Rajputs and in the second onslaught his troops led by Kutb-ud-din succeeded in taking Delhi, whose sultanate thereafter took a certain degree of precedence over the Indian principalities.

From then on the Muslim princes and generals launched campaign after campaign; new dynasties were founded, new kingdoms established, followed in some cases by ruthless persecution of unbelievers, and the new kingdoms bit deeper and deeper into the Hindu principalities in the Deccan. A new class of warriors with their families and their own social structure emerged in the midst of the Hindus, who fought hard to defend their caste laws. There were now two Indias. To the Indian temples with their rich imagery were added Islamic tombs, mosques, minarets and palaces, with their distinctive script and abstract ornaments.

At the end of the fourteenth century the conqueror of Central Asia, Timur, also invaded India, occupied Delhi, but then moved on again. His descendant Babur, who also claimed descent from the great Genghis Khan, after conquering Delhi in 1526 founded a dynasty which was to be the most powerful in India since that of the Buddhist emperors and it seemed, in fact, as if his grandson, Akbar, had inherited something of the spirit of Asoka: this pious Moslem ruler not only practised tolerance, but in his later years proclaimed a universal religion, which, he hoped, would resolve the religious differences among his peoples. For two hundred years the Mogul dynasty ruled the great empire between the Himalayas and the Deccan. The bigotted Aurangzeb, sixth in succession to Babur, managed somehow to hold the reins of the empire in his bony fingers, but after he had gone the power of the Grand Mogul remained no more than a legend.

But the Mogul Empire was not India. In the Deccan there were four sultanates, which succeeded, by joining forces, in overthrowing the powerful Hindu emperor of Vijayanagar in 1565. It was there, in the seventeenth century, that Shivaji founded his own Mahratta state and gave the Hindu community a new sense of mission. In the Punjab a new religious community, the Sikhs, had emerged, and they too, in the struggle to assert themselves, became a military and political power. But the credit for unifying the whole of India was to fall to a very different power, which employed entirely new methods, pursued quite different aims and brought a new message to the country.

The new masters had already gained footholds in various parts of India. The Portuguese, who landed at Calicut in 1498 and occupied Goa in 1510, brought the message of Christianity. But their primary concern was trade. Then came the Dutch, the English and the French. For a time there was some doubt whether the French or the English were in a stronger position, but then the great Duplessis was recalled to Paris and the charter granted by Elizabeth I to a group of London merchants giving them a trading monopoly with India enabled the East India Company to expand steadily and systematically into a major enterprise which Great Britain was prepared to defend with all her power. In 1639-40 the English obtained the permission of the king of Vijayanagar to build a fort in Madras. Bombay, which the king of Gujarat had handed over to the Portuguese in 1534, became the property of the king of England by marriage in 1665 and he passed it on to the East India Company. In the Bengal delta of the Ganges and the Brahmaputra, where the Portuguese had been trading since 1537, the English built their first factory in 1651, and in 1690, with the permission of the Nawab of Bengal, they started fortifying Calcutta, which in the eighteenth century became their main base in India.

When the English came to India, it was not with any intention to conquer territory or found an empire. With characteristic pragmatism they took stock of the situation, opened up new markets for the industries that were springing up at home and were not afraid to employ military or political weapons to develop and consolidate London's position as a centre of world trade. India was a medley of rival states, which the English played off one against the other, allying themselves today with one prince, tomorrow with another, until they themselves emerged as the sole arbiter. Thus the warlike Mahrattas, Sikhs and Rajputs, who had been both friends and foes, ended by submitting to British supremacy and becoming the *élite* of the Anglo-Indian army.

In 1774 Warren Hastings was installed in Calcutta as the first governor general, ten years later, with the passing of Pitt's India Act, control was transferred to the government and parliament in Westminster, but it was not until 1858, following the Indian Mutiny of 1857, that the British Crown itself assumed responsibility for the administration of the Company. The governor general became viceroy and from then on the Indians were subjects of Her Britannic Majesty, who, in 1877 when Disraeli was prime minister, became empress of India. In December 1911 a British monarch stepped for the first and only time on Indian soil, when King George V was crowned emperor of India and announced that the capital of the empire would be transferred from Calcutta, where the viceroy had formerly resided, to Delhi.

It had never occurred to the English that they should follow the example of so many immigrants and conquerors before them and become Indians. The possibility was never even considered that the king-emperor might take up residence in Calcutta or Delhi; he remained a foreign ruler, which meant that there was always something provisional about the Anglo-Indian empire: despite all New Delhi's proud monuments, the shrewd English knew in their hearts that they could only play a limited part in this great subcontinent. This knowledge is reflected in the words of one of the greatest exponents of British imperialism, Lord Curzon, after he had retired as viceroy (1898-1905). They might well serve as a fitting epitaph to British rule in Inida:

A hundred times in India have I said to myself, O that to every Englishman in this country, as he ends his work, might be truthfully applied the phrase 'Thou has loved righteousness and hated iniquity'. No man has, I believe, ever served India faithfully of whom that could not be said. All other triumphs are tinsel and sham. Perhaps there are few of us who make anything but a poor approximation to that ideal. But let it be our ideal all the same. To fight for the right, to abhor the imperfect, the unjust or the mean, to swerve neither to the right hand nor to the left, to care nothing for flattery or applause or odium or abuse—it is so easy to have any of them in India—never to let your enthusiasm be soured or your courage grow dim, but to remember that the Almighty has placed your hand on the greatest of his ploughs, in whose furrow the natives of the future are germinating and taking shape, to drive the blade a little forward in your time, and to feel that somewhere among these millions you have left a little justice or happiness or prosperity, a sense of manliness or moral dignity, a spring of patriotism, a dawn of intellectual enlightenment, or a stirring of duty, where it did not before exist—that is enough, that is the Englishman's justification in India. It is good enough for his watchword while he is here, for his epitaph when he is gone.

When the British left India in 1947, independence did not fall into her lap, as it had done in the case of other countries, as an almost automatic consequence of the Second World War; on the contrary, it was a development that had been expected for some considerable time and it marked the end of decades of struggle. It is not for us here to judge how much good or how much harm the British did to India or whether they left too early or too late. A neutral observer may well remark on the fact, however, that a strange love-hate relationship persisted throughout this long struggle and that even in India today there are many things that remind one of the heritage left by the British. No Indian wants to return to the pre-colonial era and each one in his own way is adapting himself to the world civilization of today. India is no longer prepared to let her princes or her priests think for her. It may be that the struggle for independence only really began in earnest with the proclamation of the republic; for it is easier to shake off a foreign rule than it is to break oneself of the habits of centuries. The very sense of mission which India's great spiritual heritage has generated is in peril, for it is not always compatible with the needs of a modern state, and the new India's greatest leaders were aware of this. The history of India's struggle for independence is to a large extent identical with the development of the Indian National Congress, which came to power in 1947 as a well-organized party with the overwhelming support of the people.

In its early days hardly anyone in the Congress seriously thought of setting up an independent state. A former British member of the Indian Civil Service, Allan Octavian Hume, was anxious to create some kind of organization which would improve social conditions in India. The viceroy himself, Lord Dufferin, instructed him to make it a political body, for as representative of the British Crown he found he had practically no means of gauging the true feelings of the people and he therefore welcomed the establishment of an unofficial body which could act as an intermediary between people and government. The first Congress meeting in 1885 under the chairmanship of W. C. Bannerjee ended with three cheers for Hume and for Her Imperial Majesty Queen Victoria. By the following year the number of delegates had risen from seventy-two to several hundred and before long they had run into thousands. On many issues the delegates had widely divergent views; on the other hand, the rallying-cry 'Swaraj' (Independence) was growing in intensity and now only the method, the best way to achieve it, remained for discussion. Groups and parties were formed; a leader would suddenly appear like a meteor in the sky, only to disappear just as suddenly. The Congress was a school for politicians; not until M. K. Gandhi took over the leadership after the First World War did it become a mass movement. For the first time a political figure had emerged, who addressed himself to every Indian, even to the very poorest. It was the 'Mahatma' or 'great soul' who brought politics to the ignorant peasant, gave him self-confidence and a sense of national responsibility. In his brilliantly organized campaigns he preached revolution without violence, launched the non-cooperation movement (refusal to cooperate politically with the British regime) and a campaign of civil disobedience. A factor of supreme importance to Gandhi was India's great religious heritage but no less essential was tolerance, and his attitude to Christianity was more than tolerant. He was against any incitement to hatred: the British were to leave the country but at the same time were to remain his best friends. He also knew that there was much to be learned from the West; of all the European thinkers Ruskin with his humanitarian socialism appealed most to him. He deliberately remained aloof from the day-to-day political struggle, leaving others to organize and lead it, more particularly Jawaharlal Nehru, the son of his fellow Congress member Motilal Nehru.

Not even Gandhi, who sought to bring Untouchables as well as Muslims together into one true national community with the Hindus, could keep India united after the empire was dissolved or prevent the agonizing and bloody 'partition' that followed it. Since then a new

BRAHMA

7 INDRA

10 MAHAVIRA

11 BUDDHA

India has emerged, which is still struggling to achieve some kind of political and social stability. Its leaders are faced with problems, which are mounting and which only a supreme effort on the part of this highly-gifted nation can hope to master: to provide work and food for a fast-increasing population, to overcome chronic drought and reform agriculture, to press forward with industrialization, to withstand aggression from outside, but above all to devise some means of wedding a splendid cultural heritage to a social system that is in keeping with modern technology.

NOTES TO THE PLATES

1 Yakshi as bracket to architrave on east gate of great Stupa of Sanchi

2 Lion-capital of Asoka column at Sarnath. Archaeological Museum, Sarnath

3 Women water-carriers near Delhi

4 Vishnu, the Preserver or Penetrator, in a south Indian form as Vardaraja. Bronze of the Chola period. Central Museum, Madras

5 Mahabalipuram, Trimurti cave, Pallava period, 7th century. The central cell with the lingam, symbol of Siva, and behind it the figure of Siva

6 Brahma, four-headed god of creation; in his four hands as attributes a part of the Vedas, a spoon, a garland of roses and a water-vessel; beside him, his wife Sarasvati. Hoysala temple, early 12th century

7 Indra, Vedic god of the storm and prince of the gods, riding on his vehicle, the elephant. From Halebid, 12th century. Bangalore Museum

8, 9 Khajuraho. The Kandarya-Mahadeo (Siva) Temple, c. AD 1000. General view from the east and main entrance

10 Mahavira-Jina, founder of the Jain religion. Black basalt, c. 4th century AD; from Warangal. Hyderabad Museum

11 Buddha in the 'wheel-turning' attitude: dharma mudra i.e. teaching. Sandstone carving of the Gupta period. Archaeological Museum, Sarnath

12 On the banks of the Ganges at Benares

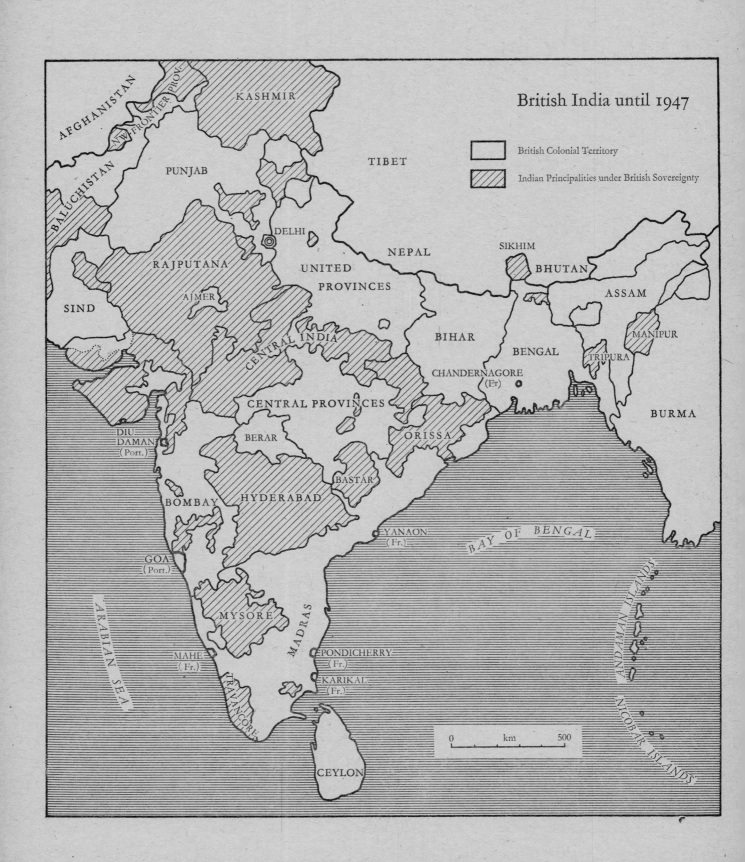

British India until 1947

British Colonial Territory

Indian Principalities under British Sovereignty

AFGHANISTAN

N.W.FRONTIER PROV.

BALUCHISTAN

KASHMIR

PUNJAB

TIBET

SIND

RAJPUTANA

AJMER

DELHI

UNITED
PROVINCES

NEPAL

SIKHIM

BHUTAN

ASSAM

CENTRAL INDIA

BIHAR

BENGAL

MANIPUR

TRIPURA

CENTRAL PROVINCES

CHANDERNAGORE
(Fr)

BERAR

ORISSA

BURMA

DIU
DAMAN
(Port.)

BASTAR

BOMBAY

HYDERABAD

GOA
(Port.)

YANAON
(Fr.)

BAY OF BENGAL

ARABIAN SEA

MYSORE

MADRAS

MAHE
(Fr.)

PONDICHERRY
(Fr.)

TRAVANCORE

KARIKAL
(Fr.)

ANDAMAN ISLANDS

NICOBAR ISLANDS

0   km   500

CEYLON

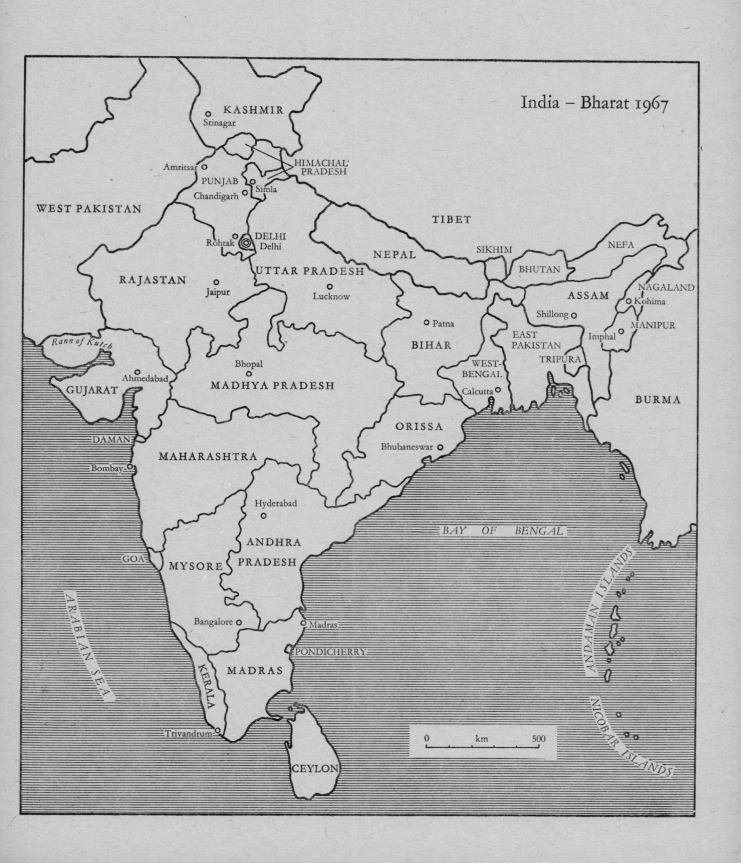

India – Bharat 1967

KASHMIR
Srinagar

Amritsar
PUNJAB
Chandigarh
Simla
HIMACHAL
PRADESH

WEST PAKISTAN

TIBET

Rohtak
DELHI
Delhi

NEPAL

SIKHIM

NEFA

BHUTAN

NAGALAND
Kohima

ASSAM

MANIPUR

Shillong

Imphal

RAJASTAN

UTTAR PRADESH

Jaipur

Lucknow

Patna

Rann of Kutch

BIHAR

EAST
PAKISTAN

TRIPURA

WEST-
BENGAL

Ahmedabad

Bhopal

GUJARAT

MADHYA PRADESH

Calcutta

BURMA

DAMAN

ORISSA

MAHARASHTRA

Bombay

Bhubaneswar

Hyderabad

BAY OF BENGAL

ANDAMAN ISLANDS

ANDHRA
PRADESH

GOA

MYSORE

ARABIAN SEA

Bangalore

Madras

PONDICHERRY

NICOBAR ISLANDS

KERALA

MADRAS

Trivandrum

0   km   500

CEYLON

INDIAN DYNASTIES and the buildings erected in their reigns

MAURYA 322–185 BC
Chandragupta, *c.* 322–298 BC
Palace of Pataliputra

ASOKA 273–232 BC
Inscribed columns, e.g. in Sarnath, Stupas, etc.

SUNGA 185–73 BC
Bharhut Stupa, stone-railing at Bodh Gaya

ANDHRA 72 BC–AD 320
Gates of the great stupa at Sanchi, caves at Nasik, early caves at Ajanta (early Andhra period). Stupas at Nagarjunakonda and Amaravati (late Andhra period)

KUSHAN AD 48–250
School of sculpture at Mathura

GUPTA AD 320–499
Caves at Badami, Caves and frescoes at Ajanta, Temple at Aihole, Sculptures at Sarnath and Mathura

PALLAVA (Kanchipuram) 2nd–10th centuries
Narasimhavarman I, called Mahamalla 625–45
Rathas at Mahabalipuram

CHALUKYA 6th–8th centuries and 973–1190
Vikramaditya II
Virupaksha temple at Pattadakal, 740

RASHTRAKUTA 8th century—973
Dantidurga 725–55
Kailasa temple at Ellora

CHOLA 9th century—1310
Rajaraja 985–1014
Temples at Tanjore and Gangaikonda Cholapuram

HOYSALA-BALLALA 12th–14th centuries
Vishnuvardhana 1111–41
Temples at Belur and Halebid

HINDU KINGDOM OF ORISSA 5th–16th centuries
Lelat Indra Kesari 617–57
Linguraja temple at Bhubanesar (extended in 11th century)
Narasimha Deva, 1238–64
Surya temple at Konarak

CHANDEL (Bundelkhand) 10th–11th centuries
Dhanga, 954–1002 (or 1008)
Kandariya-Mahadeo temples at Khaiuraho

VIJAYANAGAR 1336–1529
Harihara I, 1336–54
Foundation of Vijayanagar
Krishna Deva, 1509–29
Vithoba temple, Narsingh statue

THE SLAVE-SULTANS OF DELHI 1206–1290
Kutb-ud-din Aibak, 1206–10
Foundation of Quwwat-ul-Islam and Kutb Minar
Iltutmish (Altamsh), 1211–36
Buildings at Lal Kot (Old Delhi) and Ajmir

TUGHLAK SULTANS OF DELHI 1320–1414
Ghyas-ud-din Tughlak, 1320–25
Fort and tomb at Tughlakabad
Firoz Shah Tughlak, 1351–88
Mosque at Khirki, Tomb at Hauz-i-khas

LODI SULTANS OF DELHI 1451–1526
Sikandar Lodi, 1489–1517
Tomb in Old Delhi

SUR (Afghan) DYNASTY OF DELHI 1538–55
Sher Shah, 1538–45
Purana Qila (Old Delhi), tomb at Sasaram

MOGUL SULTANS OF DELHI 1526–1857
Babur, 1526–30
Foundation of the fort at Agra
Humayun, 1530–56
Tomb in Old Delhi
Akbar, 1556–1605
Palace at Agra, Fatehpur Sikri, Tomb at Sikandra
Jahangir, 1605–27
Tomb Itimat-ud-Daula Agra
Shah Jahan, 1628–57 (died 1666)
Palaces at Agra and Delhi, Taj Mahal, Ajmir
Aurangzeb, 1658–1707
Tomb Rabia Daurani near Aurangabad

TOMAR OF GWALIOR 1398–1526
Man Singh, 1486–1516
Palaces

MEWAR-UDAIPUR 8th–20th centuries
Chitor, 12th century. Lake Pichola, late 14th century
Rana Kumbha
Victory Tower at Chitor, 1458–68
Maharana Udai Singh
Foundation of Udaipur, 1567

GHOR AND KHILJI OF MANDU 1401–1564
Hoshang Shah Ghori, 1405–35
Jama Masjid and tomb at Mandu

SULTANS OF GUJARAT 1396–1572
Ahmed Shah I, 1411–41
Foundation of Ahmedabad

NAWABS AND KINGS OF OUDH 1722–1856
Asaf-ud-Daula, 1775–97
Great Imambara at Lucknow

SIKHS AND SIKH KINGDOM
1. Guru Baba Nanak, 1469–1538
4. Guru Ram Das, 1574–81
Foundation of the Shrine at Amritsar
9. Guru Teg Bahadur, 1664–75
Foundation of Anandpur
Maharaja Ranjit Singh, 1780–1839
Foundation of Sikh Kingdom, Extension of Amritsar

THE EUROPEANS IN INDIA

1498 First landing by Vasco da Gama at Calicut.
1502 Pope Alexander VI authorizes the king of Portugal to assume the title 'Master of the shipping, conquests and trade in Egypt, Arabia, Persia and India'. The Portuguese build the first factory at Cochin.
1509–15 Alfonso d'Albuquerque becomes 'Governor of India' in Cochin.
1510 Portuguese occupy Goa.
1530 Goa becomes residence of Portuguese Viceroy.
1541–52 Francis Xavier in India.
1560 By a Charter of 31 December The 'Governor and Company of Merchants of London Trading into the East Indies' (London East India Company) is granted the monopoly of England's trade with India for an initial period of fifteen years.
1602 United East Indies Company of the Netherlands is founded.
1612 Danish East Indies Company is founded.
1639 Fort St George at Madras built by the English.
1651 First English factory built on the Hooghli in Bengal.
1661 Portugal cedes Bombay to England.
1664 Colbert founds the Compagnie des Indes.
1674 François Martin establishes a French base at Pondicherry.
1690 Foundation of Calcutta.
1698 Foundation of English East India Company which amalgamates with London East India Company in 1702.
1742–54 Dupleix Governor of Pondicherry. Peak period of French power in India.
1784 Pitt's India Act defines relationship between the Company and the British Crown and confirms the senior status of the Governor General of Bengal.
1803 Lord Lake occupies Delhi.
1824 Holland cedes her possessions to Britain.
1835 English becomes the official language in the areas controlled by the British.
1845 Denmark cedes her possessions to Britain.
1857 The Sepoy Mutiny is crushed by the British.
1858 British Crown takes over the government of India.
1869 Opening of the Suez Canal.
1876 Queen Victoria is proclaimed Empress of India.
1909 The Morley-Minto Reforms provide for Indian participation in government.
1911 George V is crowned emperor in Delhi and announces that Delhi is the new capital.
1921 The Montagu-Chelmsford Reforms provide for increased participation in government by the native population.
1935 The Government of India Bill gives the provinces complete autonomy.
1947 On 15 August the Anglo-Indian Empire is dissolved and the government handed over to representatives of the Indian people.
1961 Indian troops occupy Goa and liquidate Portuguese possessions in India.
1962 Pondicherry and other French possessions are ceded to India.

MADRAS

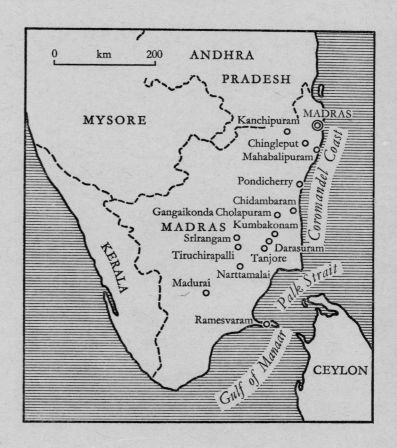

When the traveller arriving from the south, from Ceylon for example, first sets foot on Indian soil, he immediately finds himself in a world dominated by Hinduism; for here, more than anywhere else in India, Hinduism is a way of life, and in the course of the centuries temple after temple has been built to the glory of the Hindu gods. At the beginning of the fourteenth century, it is true, Malik Kafur, one of the sultan of Delhi's generals, led his plundering army right down the Coromandel Coast as far south as Madurai and Rameswaram, later Aurangzeb occupied the holy city of Kanchipuram, and the Muslim rulers of the Deccan also made their presence felt; but by and large the Tamil-speaking area of the modern state of Madras, which covers only a part of the former Madras Presidency, remained, unlike other parts of India, almost exclusively Hindu.

As is so often the case with Hinduism, we know precious little about the dynasties which ruled here over kingdoms that had periods of great power and prosperity, and although the names of certain rulers are known from inscriptions, there are still many gaps which the historian can only fill by drawing on his imagination.

In ancient times the native Dravidians, who were a seafaring people, had established trading relations with the Mediterranean countries and presumably also with Indonesia. They remained outside the Mauryan Empire but the Brahmanism of the Indo-Aryans bringing the spiritual message of the Vedas had penetrated even this far south, to be followed by Buddhism and, most successful of all, the religion of the Jains.

The Chinese traveller, Hiuen-tsang (629–645), a reliable reporter, describes how on his journey southwards he came to a land called 'Chola' (Chu-li-ye), whose capital looked barren and deserted; this can hardly have been the land of the Chola dynasty, for he travelled a considerable distance further south before he reached Kanchipuram, the centre of the Pallava kingdom which was still some way to the north of the Chola territory. He calls this land with its famous holy city 'Dravida' (Ta-lo-pi-ch'a) and describes it, by contrast with the country he had previously travelled through, as 'fertile and well-administered', an impression which one still has today. He is full of praise for the inhabitants: 'They are courageous, set great store by honesty and truth, and

honour learning'. He also found several hundred monasteries, where the holy scriptures of northern India were used. This was during the reign of Narasimhavarman, better known by his dynastic name, Mahamalla. Although the Chinese traveller gives us to understand that he had arrived in a Buddhist country, there is no doubt that Hinduism was at least regaining its hold, and for centuries to come the 'golden city' Kanchipuram (also called Conjeeveram) was to remain its spiritual centre and the birthplace of a rich religious literature emanating from the worship of Vishnu and Siva. But Mahamalla's name is also linked with the building of a holy place of pilgrimage Mahabalipuram (or Mamallapuram) on the coast not far from the capital, where the most magnificent examples of early south Indian art could be seen: rock-temples and caves, richly sculptured, were hewn out of the granite rock which one finds throughout the southern Deccan—the few illustrations in this book can give only a very incomplete picture of the great architectural variety of that period, even in less durable materials, and of the lavish sculptures. The outstanding example is the relief entitled 'The descent of Ganga' or 'Aryuna's penance', which is almost a hundred feet long and over forty feet high: gods, men and animals, dominated by the figure of Siva, unite to give thanks in a feast of peace for the blessings bestowed by the waters of the Ganges. Presumably the rock-crevice representing the Ganges, from which the Naga king with the snake's body is seen emerging, was originally washed by the water that emerged from the rock-face. If one had to choose one out of all the treasures that India has to offer, it would undoubtedly be this particular masterpiece with its unique artistic as well as human appeal.

There was a long and bitter rivalry between the Pallavas on the one hand and, on the other, the dynasties of the Cholas and in the extreme south the Pandyas. The Cholas established a massive empire which in the eleventh century covered the whole of southern India and which saw the second golden age of Dravidian architecture and sculpture. The finest examples are the Brihadiswara temple at Tanjore with its 220 feet high tower over the sanctuary, the temple of Gangaikonda Cholapuram, which is much less frequented but is a gem of plastic art, and the sea-girt 'Shore Temple' at Mahabalipuram. The

15 MAHABALIPURAM: SHIVA, PARVATI

16 MAHABALIPURAM: ANANTASAYI VISHNU

Chola period also produced the finest religious images in bronze, the most impressive collection of which is in the Madras Museum.

The visitor to southern India, however, is particularly impressed by the great temples with their high, lavishly-sculptured 'gopurams' (towers over the gateways), which are relatively recent constructions. The connoisseur may speak rather disparagingly of their plastic sculpture and maintain that it lacks the clarity and expressive power which the Pallava and Chola artists put into their work, but just as Gothic and Romantic, Baroque and Renaissance art can flourish side by side, so too the temples of Madurai (generally known as Madura in Europe), Kumbakonam, Chidambaram, Srirangam and Rameswaram, to mention only a few of the most impressive examples, offer a truly breathtaking profusion of plastic artistry, and what they lack in detailed craftsmanship they make up for in the splendour and complexity of the overall composition. It must be borne in mind that there was less scope for developing new styles than in Europe, with its zest for innovation. The basic iconographic forms were prescribed—one can see this in the many sculptures of Siva as Nataraja (Lord of the Dance) preserved in various museums—but each period also developed its own style and there were master-sculptors to guide the hands of the craftsmen.

Madurai, the metropolis of the Tamil culture as well as the seat of the Pandya rulers, became part of the empire of Vijayanagar in the fourteenth century; in the second half of the sixteenth century its governor, Visvanatha, founded the Nayak dynasty, but it was Tirumal Nayak (1623–59), the great builder of Madurai, who finally succeeded in shaking off the last vestiges of Pandya, after the empire of Vijayanagar had already collapsed.

In the centre of the city stands the Minakshi temple. Legend has it that, in answer to a prayer by the childless King Malayadhwaja of Madurai to Siva, a child was born from the sacrificial fire and that this child was the 'fish-eyed' goddess Minakshi. The royal couple's joy was clouded by the fact that their daughter had three breasts. A celestial apparition revealed to them that the third breast would disappear as soon as Minakshi found her husband. When her parents died, the princess, who had barely come of age, ascended the throne. There followed a series of military campaigns in which she defeated all earthly rulers and even the Lords of Heaven, not excluding the God of Thunder, Indra; but when she came face to face with Siva himself, her third breast immediately disappeared and the princess recognized her lord and master. So Siva came down to earth as Sundara Pandaya or Sundareshvara, was formally married and ruled as king, bringing blessings upon the country, until his son was ready to succeed him and, together with Minakshi, he cast off his earthly body. Each of the two godheads has a separate shrine in the heart of the temple. As in so many of these large temples, the original sanctuary is surrounded by a pool and by a succession of pillared halls, courtyards and towered gateways—no less than nine gopurams, the largest being the outer gateways, which are covered with row upon row of sculptured figures and, lit at night by thousands of electric bulbs, proclaim to the world at large the glory of the gods. Only a short time ago the faded columns were given a fresh coat of bright paint (the great temple of Kumbakonam with its eleven-storey gopuram was given the same treatment)—and while the aesthetes may have been shocked, the Brahmans were delighted. Opposite the temple is the hall known as Tirumal's Choultry, which King Tirumal had built in 1623–45; with its dynastic statues, which can be identified on the pillars amidst mythical animals, dancers and other figures, it is a sort of pantheon for a dynasty of which little other trace is left in India's recorded history.

Even vaster is the Vishnu temple of Srirangam, which the Nayaks built on an island in the river Kaveri near Tiruchirapalli: seven encircling walls, the outermost a rectangle of a thousand by eight hundred yards, surround the heart of the temple, which was built at an earlier date and which is, in fact, a busy town, in which the fourth wall with its great gopurams encloses the temple proper.

There are very few places where one of the two main gods of later Hinduism is worshipped alone, so not far from Vishnu's temple there is also a temple of Siva, where he is worshipped as Jambukeswar—a somewhat smaller, quieter building, but its pillared halls, despite the oppressive splendour of the sculpture, have an air of solemn dignity. In the shrine the water-lingam is worshipped, one of the eight murti (avatars) in which Siva manifests himself.

Perhaps the most splendid halls are the corridors, covering altogether 1300 yards, which surround the shrine of Rameswaram at the entrance to 'Adam's Bridge' on the threshold of Ceylon. Rama himself, the heroic incarnation of Vishnu and hero of the Ramayana, is said to have built this shrine in honour of Siva, when he was bound for Ceylon in search of Sita, his wife—so here again we find the two godheads worshipped side by side.

A characteristic feature of the temples in southern India is the pool, and sometimes one also finds a rectangular pool, often with a small island-temple in the middle, outside the main temple or on the outskirts of the town. Thus the city of Kumbakonam, apart from its eighteen temples, also has the famous Mahamakham Pool, which is surrounded by pavilions and flights of steps. Once every twelve years in some miraculous way the waters of the sacred Ganges are said to flow in here instead of the Kaveri and so great is the throng of bathing pilgrims at that time that the level of the water rises visibly.

Finally there is the temple of Nataraja at Chidambaram, which has a splendour all its own.

Of the three great dances of Siva one is an evening dance in the Himalayas, which is described as follows in one of the hymns:

> The mother of the three worlds seated on a golden throne, radiant in the most magnificent jewels, Sulapani dances on the summit of Mount Kailasa, and all the gods are assembled round him: Sarasvati plays the vina, Brahma beats time on the cymbal, Lakshmi sings, Vishnu beats the drum, and all the Gandharas, Yakshas, Patagas, Uragas, Siddhas, Sadhyas, Vidyadharas, Amaras, Apsaras, all creatures of the three worlds sit round in wonderment, admiring the dance and the divine choir.

When Siva performs the 'Tandava' dance, he is Bhairavi, the Terrible. It is the dance of terror and destruction, performed in cremation grounds. In the Tandava the whole world will one day disappear and Siva, whose insatiable creative urge finds its expression in the dance, will bring forth a new universe.

The Nadanta, on the other hand, which Siva dances as Nataraja, is performed in the golden hall of Chidambaram. In the town of Chidambaram on the banks of the Sabhapati a prince once saw the god dancing in the dusk with Parvati at his side, and he built a splendid temple on that spot (tenth century AD). Nataraja also appeared dancing to individual holy men at various times thereafter. In the course of the centuries (until the end of the seventeenth) the temple was extended to become one of the largest in India, with towered gateways covered with sculptured figures, vast halls whose walls are decorated with reliefs, shrines dedicated to various gods, and a large pool for ritual bathing; at the heart of the temple, in the holiest of holies, approached by five silver steps and covered by a gilded roof, stands the statue of Nataraja, and behind a curtain is one of the five most sacred lingams—and the most remarkable of them all—the 'air-lingam', which no human eye has ever seen in any way other than through belief in the soul as a mirror of the supernatural.

NOTES TO THE PLATES

13 Siva as Natesha or Nataraja (Lord of the Dance), surrounded by a wreath of flame, performing the cosmic dance Nadanta. Bronze sculpture of the Chola period. Central Museum, Madras

14 Mahabalipuram (also Mamallapuram or Mahavelipur). The Seashore Temple of the 8th century

15 Mahabalipuram. Siva and Parvati. Bas relief in the central shrine of the Seashore Temple

16 Mahabalipuram. Yamapuri or Mahishamardini Mandapam, Durga's cave, 7th century. High-relief with Vishnu sleeping on the snake Sesa

17 Madurai, Minaksi Temple. The southern gopuram (gate-tower), about 160 ft high, with its multitude of 17th-century sculptures; these were repainted around 1960

18, 19 Rameswaram. Round what was once the heart of the Great Temple, where the lingam attributed to Rama is cooled daily with Ganges water, runs a 4000 ft long corridor with fantastically decorated columns, a masterpiece from the later period of Dravidian temple-building

20 A Brahman, recognizable by the white cord strung round his body, with his pupils in the temple at Rameswaram

21 The rock-temple of Tiruparankunram near Madurai

22 In one of the corridors of the Minaksi Temple at Madurai

23 Madurai, Minaksi Temple. Column in the Hall of a Thousand Columns showing Sarasvati, Brahma's wife, riding on a peacock

24 Madurai. Pudu Mandapam or Tirumala's Choultry, a hall built by King Tirumala, 1623–45, opposite the Minaksi Temple with statues of Tirumala and other rulers, surrounded by mythological figures

25 Tiruchirapalli (formerly Trichinopoly or, in abbreviated form, Trichi). Above the town stands the citadel rock, crowned by a 17th century temple

26 Tiruchirapalli. Coppersmith

27 Sitanavashal. Jain cave from the reign of the Pallava king Mahendravarman (640–70) before his conversion to the Siva cult. In the entrance hall the statue of a Tirthankara. In the cave are well-preserved wall- and roof-paintings

28 Kanchipuram (Conjeeveram). Kailasa Temple with figures from the Pallava period. The group presum-

ably represents twelve wise men listening to Siva's teaching

29 Tiruchirapalli. Cave temple from the Pallava period at the southern foot of the citadel rock

30 Gangaikonda Cholapuram, Brihadisvara Temple. Figure of Chandushanugraha on the east side

31 Gangaikonda Cholapuram, Brihadisvara Temple. Ardhanarisvara, form of Siva as half-woman, half-man, on the south side

32 Gangaikonda Cholapuram, Brihadisvara Temple. Figure at the east entrance

33 Gangaikonda Cholapuram. The Brihadisvara Temple of the Chola period, seen from the north-east

34 Narttamalai. The Vijayala Temple from the Chola period

35 Darasuram near Kumbakoram. The Airavatesvara Temple from the Chola period, seen from the south-east

36 Darasuram, Airavatesvara Temple. The figure of Siva in the lingam on the west side of the shrine

37 Tanjore (Thanjavur). Tower, which served as an arsenal, in the palace built by the Nayak kings from the 16th century onwards and later extended by the Marathas

38 Madurai. Courtyard of King Tirumala Nayak's palace, showing Saracen influence

39 Kumbakonam. The Mahamakkam Tank, surrounded by 16 pavilions, is reputed to fill up with Ganges water every 12 years, when it attracts many pilgrims

40 Kumbakonam. The eleven-storey gopuram and a pavilion at the entrance to the Temple of Vishnu-Sarangapani, showing the U-shaped sign which worshippers of Vishnu paint on their foreheads. The figures carved on the temple, like those at Madurai, were repainted in glowing colours

41 Tanjore. The Brihadisvara Temple, dedicated to Siva and called the Great Pagoda, was built c. AD 1000 by Rajaraja Deva Chola and is one of the finest examples of the Chola style. It is surrounded by a wall and moats. The tower (vimana) over the shrine is 215 ft high

42 Tanjore. The Temple of Subrahmaya, god of war and son of Siva, was built in the 18th century within the precincts of the Brihadisvara Temple

19–20 RAMESVARAM

21 TIRUPARANKUNRAM
22–23 MADURAI

21

22

23

25–26 TIRUCHIRAPALLI

27 SITANAVASHAL

28 KANCHIPURAM

29 TIRUCHIRAPALLI
30–33 GANGAIKOND
CHOLAPURAM

31

32

33

36

34 NARTTAMALAI
35-36 DARASURAM

37 TANJORE

38 MADURAI

39 KUMBAKONAM

43

44

45

46

48

49

47 SRIRANGAM
48 TIRUKKALI-
KUNDRAM
49 CHIDAMBARAM

52

52-55
CHINGLEPUT
56-59
MAHABALIP

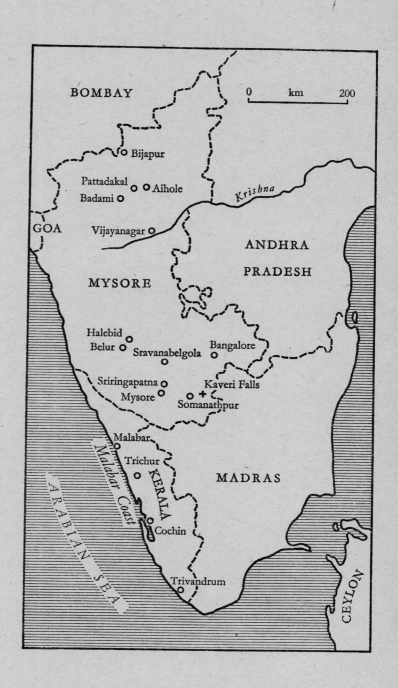

BOMBAY

0   km   200

Bijapur

Pattadakal ○ ○ Aihole

Badami ○

GOA

Krishna

Vijayanagar ○

ANDHRA

PRADESH

MYSORE

Halebid ○
Belur ○   ○ Sravanabelgola   Bangalore ○

Sriringapatna ○   Kaveri Falls
Mysore ○   +
Somanathpur

Malabar
Trichur ○

KERALA   MADRAS

Malabar Coast

Cochin ○

ARABIAN SEA

Trivandrum ○

CEYLON

THE STATE OF MYSORE, in which the predominant language is Kanarese, came into being when parts of the former Madras Presidency and of Hyderabad were handed over to the Maharaja of Mysore, one of the most progressive rulers in the 'native states', which, though under British sovereignty, were largely autonomous. The Buddhist and Muslim empires of northern India maintained garrisons here at various times, but the historical and cultural pattern in this part of India was derived from the Hindu dynasty of the Hoysalas and the rulers of Vijayanagar, who were the last to unite the whole of southern India in one great empire.

The Hoysalas made their appearance at the beginning of the eleventh century in an area which had belonged to the Chola empire but in part also to the Chalukyas from the north. The Hoysalas reached the peak of their power under Vishnuvardhana (1111–41). In his capital Dorasamudra, now called Halebid (i.e. the old City), and in the nearby city of Belur his architect and sculptor Janak Acharya built the magnificent temples whose sculptures made Hoysala art famous: fragments of this work that have found their way into museums clearly show the characteristic delight in intricate ornamentation, and the lichen-like motifs which serve as a framework in which the entire Hindu iconography is displayed. Here again the principal gods are seen in peaceful coexistence: at Belur, Siva appears in many forms, as a dancer or with his wife Parvati and Nandi the bull, and at Halebid the friezes in the Vishnu temple tell the story of the Ramayana, every episode of which is familiar to the Indians. On one of the richly-decorated crossbeams at Belur is a sculpture of the royal founder himself. The third Hoysala masterpiece is at Somanathpur and is attributed to the same builders, but, according to an inscription, it was not completed until 1270; here, in addition to the sculptures, one must admire in particular the superb architectural design of the temple with its towers built over the three shrines on a star-shaped base.

On one relief at Belur a Tirthankara is depicted, indicating that it was planned to build a Jain temple here. But during the construction the ruler became a devout Hindu and adopted the name of the god, Vishnu, whom he most revered. Disciples of the Jain teaching, who at one time were so influential in this area, still have their own holy place at Sravanabelgola not far from Belur. In the fourth century BC a famous sage named Bhadra Bahu lived here and, so tradition has it, was given instruction in the Jain teaching by one of the six pupils of Mahavira. The founder of the Mauryan Empire, Asoka's grandfather Chandragupta, is said to have come here after abdicating his throne in order to spend his last years in the holy man's company. In the year 983 the Jain monolith, fifty-five feet high, was erected on the Indragiri rock, where it is visible far across the plain as it towers over the walls of the temple surrounding it, its face turned northwards. Like other Jain figures, the statue is naked and a plant has entwined itself around it as it stands in mute meditation. According to the inscription, it represents Gomata Raya, the younger of two sons of a ruler, who fought a duel to decide the succession; after Gomata had emerged victorious, he surrendered the throne to his defeated brother and led the life of a saint.

The capital of the Hoysalas was plundered by Malik Kafur in 1310, in 1326 it was once again overrun by the Muslims, and with the death at the age of eighty-five of Vira Ballala III, who was slain on the battlefield by the ruler of Madurai, no more is heard of the dynasty. Its place was taken by the Vijayanagar Empire, the origins of which are shrouded in the mists that cover so much of India's history. And the origins of the first three dynasties of Vijayanagar are also obscured by the confusion that so frequently arose over Hindu successions. The son did not always succeed the father; often it was the younger brother who succeeded the elder. Amongst the statesmen, generals and scholars—functions that were frequently performed by one and the same person—there were groups of two or more brothers. We are constantly hearing of powerful ministers and governors who had married into the royal house and acted as personal advisers and friends to the ruler. Time and again a distinguished family, represented by a series of brothers, seized the reins of government, when the ruler's hold on them had weakened, and sooner or later claimed the throne; this is what seems to have happened with the founders of Vijayanagar. The troops of the sultan of Delhi, Muhammad Tughlak, which advanced as far as the banks of the Tungabhadra, are said to have recalled the governor they had left behind in Aregundi and to have handed over the administration to a minister of the Hindu

66
67

68
69

prince Deva Raya. The raya (the southern Indian word for raja or prince) arranged a meeting on the river-bank opposite Anegundi with a wise man named Madhava Charya, better known as Vidyaranya or Forest of Knowledge, who advised him to build a city on that spot, where, it seems, the shrine of Hampi already stood. It may be, on the other hand, that the city had already been built by the last Hoysala king, for the river formed a natural defence against the northern invaders. One thing seems definite, that, when the troops of the mighty ruler of Delhi withdrew, five sons of a certain Sangama governed that territory, either in the name of the Hoysala kings or as vassals of the kingdom of Warangal, which was also threatened by the Muslims (and which, after the defeat of 1327, nevertheless managed to survive until 1425).

The first of the five brothers, Harihara I, who had presumably been governing the territory of Goa, is generally regarded as the founder of the first dynasty. He is mentioned by Ibn Batuta, who travelled in India about this time, and the reports of this famous Arab mark the beginning of a more regular flow of historical material, more so than for any Hindu empire before. After seven years Harihara was succeeded by his younger brother, Bukka I, and about the same time the Muslim, Ala-ud-din, whose surname was Bahman, founded the Bahmani kingdom in the Deccan, which throughout its entire existence (until 1525) was in a state of almost constant war with Vijayanagar. In the campaigns launched by both sides the population, including women and children, was indiscriminately massacred, till the rather more peaceable Muhammad Shah (1358–73) came to an agreement with Bukka that non-combatants should be spared—a humane gesture which was remarkable in such a day and age; for, despite the gentle teaching of the Hindu religion, the warriors of Vijayanagar were no less ferocious than their adversaries, and indeed it seems to have been they who resumed the senseless massacres and devastations after some fifty years of restraint.

The kingdom of Vijayanagar was destined to halt the advance of Islam in the Deccan and to provide a safe refuge for the Brahman culture. But the confrontation took the form of a power-struggle between the kings, and the element of holy war was virtually non-existent. The eighth Bahmani sultan, Firoz (1397–1422), a particularly fierce enemy of unbelievers, had two Hindu wives and,

when he had successfully completed one of his campaigns with a peace that was humiliating for Vijayanagar, he entered his adversary's city in order to marry one of his daughters. The Hindu king, for his part, took Muslim bowmen into his service, after he had noticed how effective they were in battle, and an entire Muslim quarter with its own mosque grew up in his capital.

Under Deva Raya II, who became sole ruler in 1424, the administration of the kingdom was reorganized. Two foreign visitors have described the striking impression made upon them by the capital. The Venetian merchant, Nicola Conti, whose account was written down for the Pope by Poggio Bracciolini, estimates that it had a circumference of about sixty miles, and Abdur Razzak, ambassador of the Great Khan of Samarkand, Timur's successor, wrote:

> The city is so large that no man has seen its like upon the earth. It has seven lines of fortification one within the other. In the centre is the king's palace. Between the first, second and third walls houses have been built in the midst of cultivated fields and gardens. Between the third and the seventh walls are a host of shops and bazars. At any time of the year one can have fresh, sweet-smelling flowers, for in this place they are considered essential to life. The jewellers have their rubies and pearls and diamonds openly displayed. In the heart of the city, where the king's residence is situated, an abundant supply of water flows through channels of polished stone. In the king's treasure-house there are rooms with depressions in the floors, into which molten gold is poured. All inhabitants, whether high or low, wear jewels and golden ornaments in their ears and round their necks, arms, wrists and fingers.

That such descriptions are not necessarily indicative of the general social conditions at that gime is clear from a report by the Russian Athanasius Nikitin, who travelled through the Deccan between 1470 and 1474 and wrote: 'The country is overpopulated; living conditions on the land are very bad, while the upper class wallow in wealth and prosperity'.

Among Deva's successors Saluwa Narasingha, a man of noble birth who had married into the royal house, distinguished himself in the wars against the Hindu prince of Orissa, who had allied himself with the Muslims of Bahmani. Eventually Narasingha seized the throne from the weak ruler in 1487—this was the so-called First Usurpation, and under the new dynasty the worship of Siva was replaced by the cult of Vishnu, of which there are still monuments standing in Vijayanagar.

Narasingha ruled for six years and on his deathbed entrusted his general, Narasa, with the regency until his son Narasingha II was old enough to reign. But when Narasa died in 1505, his own son Vira Narasingha took the throne. This was the Second Usurpation and the beginning of the third dynasty. In order to ensure that one of his sons succeeded him, the king made his faithful minister Saluva Timma promise that, after his death, he would blind his younger brother who was predestined to succeed him. Timma, however, did not have the heart to commit such a crime, so Vira Narasingha's brother came to the throne with the title Krishnaraya Deva (1509–29) and proved to be the greatest of the kings of Vijayanagar. He emerged victorious from the wars against Orissa and Bahmani and consolidated his kingdom, which covered the whole of southern India from the Deccan as far as Rameswaram.

The Portuguese, Domingo Paes, in his account of 'the Narasingha Kingdom' painted a graphic picture of the city in its final heyday. He describes the King as

> of medium height and fair complexion. He commands more respect and is a more complete king than any other one can imagine. He is of a frank disposition and can be very gay. He welcomes strangers at any time and enquires after their affairs. He is a great ruler, his sense of justice is very marked, but he succumbs easily to outbursts of rage.

He is remembered for his chivalry towards defeated enemies and for his patronage of the arts and sciences. He always treated his minister Saluva Timma with the greatest respect, although this did not prevent them from quarrelling towards the end of his reign. The ruler always dressed in white, his garments embroidered with golden roses; he went barefoot and wore diamonds round his neck, while his turban of gold brocade was shaped like a Galician helmet. The king had twelve legitimate wives, three of whom were his chief wives and held equal rank, and their sons were in the direct succession. One of these wives was the daughter of the king of Orissa, another the daughter of the vassal king of Seringapatao, and the third was the daughter of a courtier, who had been Krishna's mistress before he ascended the throne and whom he had promised to marry. Each of these queens had sixty female attendants, who escorted her everywhere and on ceremonial occasions were richly bejewelled.

Paes tells us that in size the city could only be compared with Rome and that it contained more than 100,000 houses. One room in the royal palace was completely lined with ivory and the ivory pillars were carved with roses and lotus-flowers.

The king ranked as the sole landowner in the country, which was divided into some two hundred provinces and was governed in his name. Most of the towns were surrounded by mud walls; stone walls were forbidden in order to discourage any organized resistance. Punishments for theft were savage in order to maintain order and protect property. The dancing-girls from the temple lived in the finest streets, where they engaged in prostitution without anyone taking offence. Indeed, 'these women are even allowed to visit the king's wives, to chat and chew betel with them, something no one else is permitted to do'. Some were rich, and we are assured that the revenue from the brothels was sufficient to finance the twelve-thousand strong police force.

Krishna Deva's declining years were beset by illness and rebellion. His brother, Achyuta, who succeeded him in 1530, managed somehow to hold the kingdom together but he was chiefly interested in the pleasures of the flesh and left his ministers to govern. Two families, who were related to the royal house, engaged in a struggle for power, and the historian has an almost impossible task to try to sort out the confusion, particularly as the names themselves seem almost designed to confuse: two brothers, both called Tirumala, one of whom has passed into history as the mad Tirumala, proved, for a time at least, stronger than their rivals from the Araviti family, the three brothers Rama, Tirumala and Venkata. When Achyuta died in 1542, his son Venkata (not the Venkata who has just been mentioned), who had been named his successor, was murdered by the mad Tirumala, and when the murderer himself saw that the game was up, he gave orders for the royal treasure to be destroyed, the royal elephants blinded and finally took his own life. The three brothers placed Sadasiva, a nephew of the two previous kings, on the throne but saw to it that he was no more than a figure-head. The real ruler was the eldest brother, Ram Raya. He joined in the wars between the Muslim states which had sprung up with the collapse of the Bahmani kingdom; on one occasion he allied himself with Ahmadnagar against Bijapur, on another with Bijapur against Ahmadnagar, but he offended all Muslims alike with his arrogance and they finally united against him.

So in 1565 a great battle was fought at Talikot, at which the combined forces of the Deccan princes under the command of Hussain Nizam Shah of Ahmadnagar met a Hindu army of more than a million men with two thousand elephants. Ram Raya was by now a very old man—one chronicler describes him as 'ninety-six years old but courageous as a man of thirty'. He gave his brothers Tirumala and Venkata command of the right and left wings, while he himself took command of the centre, was carried into battle in a splendid litter and issued precise instructions on what was to happen to each of the defeated Muslim kings. When the victory which he had so confidently expected showed no signs of materializing, Rama mounted a throne and promised his faithful followers that victory would be rewarded with the jewels and gold and silver coins heaped around him. By the time he returned to his litter, the superior Muslim artillery had breached the centre of the Hindu army, Rama was taken prisoner and, according to one report, the Muslim leader at once struck off his head with his own hand. 100,000 Hindus, including Venkata, were left dead on the battlefield.

Of the three brothers only Tirumala escaped; he took the helpless King Sadasiva with him, and retreated to the fortress of Penukonda. Some two years later the king died—it may be that he was murdered—and Tirumala founded a new dynasty, which eventually established its capital at Chandragiri.

In the meantime the empire of Vijayanagar had disappeared and the 'City of Victory' never rose again from its ruins. But it had fulfilled its historical purpose well, for southern India remained under predominantly Hindu rule and Islamic domination of the subcontinent was averted.

To the modern visitor the atmosphere seems closer to the period when Vijayanagar was founded than to the heyday just described: the wild country with its hills covered by trees and undergrowth and with the blocks of Deccan granite strewn about like relics of a battle of the Titans seems more suited as a retreat for the solitary ascetic than for a royal residence with its courtiers and soldiers. For months it had been plundered by its conquerors and so complete was the destruction that to this day all that remains of what was once a busy city is a miserable village near the old shrine of Hampi. Anything that survived the vandals fell to ruin, until the archaeologists set about hacking away the wild vegetation and restoring such remains as they could find—this, of course, is only one of the many tasks the research worker had, and still has, to perform in this vast country. One wanders for miles through this rocky landscape and suddenly stumbles upon yet another remarkable monument, a temple, a gateway, a pavilion, part of a city wall, the gigantic statue of Vishnu in his incarnation as Narsingh Avatar with the lion's head, the royal terrace with its reliefs, and again a temple. On the banks of the Tungabhadra one finds oneself back in everyday life: a ferry consisting of round, wicker boats covered in leather, such as one still finds on the Euphrates, is making its way across to the northern bank where the fortress of Anagundi once stood.

Even the ruins are not completely deserted. People are constantly appearing, even in the wildest parts of India. They come from somewhere and they go somewhere, quietly, on their bare feet. Somewhere there is a shrine that they know of. And where there are no people, there are always monkeys romping about amongst the pillars.

To the north-west of Vijayanagar and within easy reach today of Belgaum and its airport is the former Chalukya capital, Vatapi, which is the modern town of Badami and together with Pattadakal and Aihole offers an impressive group of early Dravidian monuments. Here are some of the earliest examples of the temple architecture peculiar to the whole of southern India and Orissa, and the sculptures in the caves of Badami are among the finest specimens of early Hindu plastic art. The Chalukyas reached the peak of their power under Pulakesin II (c. 608–42), who defeated the Pallavas in the south-east and drove back the mighty Harsha in the north, the last of the great Buddhist emperors.

North of Badami lies the 'City of Victory' Bijapur, the seat of one of the Muslim kings who had joined forces to conquer Vijayanagar. Yusuf Khan, who was of Turkish origin, had acquired parts of the former Bahmani kingdom, and, after the victory at Talikot, his successors turned the capital into one of the most magnificent cities in India, whose mosques, tombs and palaces vied in splendour with those of the rulers of Delhi and Ahmedabad. Within the vast city walls with their seven gates rise the palace buildings of the citadel; a second focal point is the Great Mosque built by Ali I Adil Shah (1557–80) with its domed prayer-hall. On the western fringe of the town are the mosque and tomb of Ibrahim II Adil Shah (1580–1626), forming one of the finest groups of buildings of this kind to be seen anywhere in India. It has become known as Ibrahim Rauza, has been ascribed to a Persian architect and is particularly noted for the exquisite ornamental work on the walls at the entrance. But Bijapur is known above all for the 'Gol Gumbaz' or 'Round Dome', the tomb of Muhammad Adil Shah (1626–56), near the eastern gates. The enormous dome has a diameter of 120 feet and, until reinforced concrete was introduced, was surpassed only by St Peter's in Rome (135 feet). The tomb of Muhammad's successor, Ali II, was not completed and under his successor, the ninth and last ruler, the kingdom collapsed. Aurangzeb, while he was viceroy of the Deccan, had already attacked it and, when he became emperor, he was even more determined to destroy it, for, as a strict Sunni, the mere existence of a Shiah dynasty was a thorn in his flesh.

KERALA was created, when India was reconstituted, from the former principalities of Travancore and Cochin and the Malabar district of the Madras Presidency, thus uniting the Malayalam-speaking inhabitants of the south-west coast. Of the old Chera or Kerala kingdom, which gave the new state its name, very little is known except that in the ninth century it was absorbed by the Chola kingdom and was never revived. In another respect, however, its history is of the greatest interest, although much of it is still shrouded in mystery. Phoenician sailors are reputed to have landed here and we know from coins which have been found that there was trading with the Romans. Christianity is said to have been introduced by the Apostle Thomas himself and it had certainly gained a

foothold long before the arrival of the Portuguese. The white Jewish colony of Cochin traces its origin back to the flight from Jerusalem following the destruction of the Temple. In 1293 Marco Polo met Nestorian Christians and Jews there. And this is the only part of India where Indians of high caste were converted to Christianity—during the pre-Portuguese period; at the same time, the predominant religion remained Hinduism, which formed a powerful sect of its own here and developed its own caste system.

The first European settlement was founded by the Portuguese in Cochin in 1500. The great navigator Vasco da Gama built the first factory in what was the chief port on the Malabar coast in 1502 and he died there in 1524. In 1505 Francisco Almeyda appeared with a large fleet to take up his post as viceroy and five years later he was succeeded by the mighty Albuquerque. In 1530 St Francis Xavier, India's apostle, preached his first sermon in Cochin; in 1557 the bishop's cathedral was consecrated, and in 1577 the Society of Jesus printed the first book to appear in India. To begin with, the Portuguese did not attempt to interfere with the Christian communities they had found there and it was not until the following century, when the Inquisition reached Goa, that a ruthless conversion campaign was launched by the Roman Catholic Church. In 1635 the English gained a foothold in Cochin but in 1663 the harbour was seized by the Dutch; during their occupation trade flourished and a city emerged with a distinct Dutch character which is still discernible. In 1796 Cochin became British.

The architecture on the Malabar coast is markedly different from that of the Indian subcontinent as a whole. The buildings are usually of wood—often with polished tile walls—with large roofs, which on many of the temples are built in the form of steps and resemble buildings in the Himalayan countries and the Far East.

This coastal area at the foot of the steeply-wooded Western Ghats leaves the casual visitor with the impression of a happy country. Water, which is so scarce in many parts of India, seems to be in abundance. Travelling across the bays and backwaters one passes through dense groves of slender coconut-palms with here and there the huts of a village or occasionally the white baroque façade of a church, and boats, laden with coconuts, sail smoothly to and fro. The people give an impression of vitality and nowhere else in India are there so few illiterates. But any newspaper reader knows how deceptive such a picture of happiness and tranquillity can be, for suddenly the real problems come to the surface; the food supply is not keeping pace with the growth in population, social tensions become apparent, the struggle for true socialism the gospel of the new age, arouses popular passions, and the streets become crowded with screaming demonstrators. Kerala has become the problem child of the central government in Delhi.

NOTES TO THE PLATES

65 Indra with his wife Shaci (Indrani) in the Hoysalesvara Temple at Halebid

66 Ganesa, son of Siva, who brings good fortune—in the Chenna-Kesava Temple at Belur

67 Nataraja, the dancing Siva, at Halebid

68 Hanuman, the monkey-god and ally of Rama in the Ramayana, at Belur

69 Krishna as herdsman with his pipe, from Halebid, like the previous figures from the early 12th century (now in the Calcutta Museum)

70 The Backwaters that flow through the coconut groves on the Malabar coast near Cochin

71 On the road between Bangalore and Mysore

72 Cattle market in a village between Bangalore and Mysore

73 A sugar-cane mill at the roadside between Bangalore and Mysore

74 The Kaveri (Carwery) Falls near Sivasamudram, which are enormously swollen during the monsoon rains and since 1902 have been harnessed to a power-station

75, 76 Mysore (town). Door panels in silver and ivory with court scenes in the maharaja's palace, 18th century

77 Sriringapatna (Seringapatam), original capital of the Mysore princes. Bathing-place of a temple on the Kaveri

78 Old bridge over the Kaveri near Sriringapatna

79 Belur, Chenna-Kesava Temple. Over the entrance sits the builder, the Hoysala king Vishnu Vardhana

80 Belur, Chenna-Kesava Temple. A frieze from the first stage of construction showing a Tirthankara. During the construction, around 1133, the king was converted from the Jain faith to Vishnu worship, which is reflected in the extravagant splendour of the remaining sculptures

81 Belur, Chenna-Kesava Temple. Musicians in an unfinished frieze which shows craftsmen engaged in their occupations

82 Belur, Chenna-Kesava Temple. Detail of the richly-carved southern façade, with a frieze of elephants in the base, a characteristic feature of other Hindu temples

83 Belur, Chenna-Kesava Temple. Female figure with mirror in typical Hoysala style

84 Belur. General view of the Chenna-Kesava Temple and the east entrance

85 Somanathpur (Somnathpur) near Malvalli. The Hoysala Temple as seen from the eastern entrance-hall, with the shrines of Prasanna Channa Kesava in the centre, Gopala to the south (left) and Janardhana to the north; completed in 1270, according to an inscription, by Soma, a high official at the Hoysala court

86 Halebid. Antechamber of the Jain temple

87 Somanathpur. Base of the Hoysala temple with procession of elephants and horsemen

88 Halebid. Vishnu, on the right as Rama holding a bow, above in his incarnation as Matsya, the fish

89 The hill Indrabetta or Vindhyagiri with the shrine of Sravanabelgola, centre of the Digambara Jains

90 View from Indrabetta hill on to Sravanabelgola (*i.e.* white lake) with its temple-pool and behind it Chandragiri or Chikkabetta hill, which is also crowned by Jain temples

91 Sriringapatna. Sacred tree with stones of sacrifice, which are dedicated to the snakes

92 Sravanabelgola. The statue of Gomata Raya, about 60 ft high, erected *c.* 983 by Chamunda Raya

93 Vijayanagar. Ferry across the river Tungabhadra to Anagundi on the left bank

94 Vijayanagar. Stone frame of weighing scales

95 Vijayanagar. Ratha (monolith) in the form of a temple-carriage before the Vithoba or Vittala Temple, begun in 1513 by Krishna Deva

96 Vijayanagar. Palace building in the Zenana group

97 Vijayanagar. Reliefs with themes from the Ramayana on the 'King's Terrace'

98 Vijayanagar. The granite statue of Narsingh Avatar, erected in 1528, the incarnation of Vishnu in human form with lion's head

99 Badami. View from the cave-temples on to the town with the temple-pool and the hill beyond, covered with temples

100 Pattadakal. Papnath Temple, *c.* 700, one of the earliest examples of a Dharwar (Maharashtra) temple

101 Badami. Entrance to the third cave-temple, *c.* 450–80

102 Badami. Figure of a Dwarpal (gate-keeper) with Siva's trident to the left of the entrance to the first cave

103, 104 Badami. Figures carved on the column at the entrance to the third cave, a Vishnu temple

105 Badami. Figure of Siva with 18 arms, dancing the Tandava, to the right of the entrance to the first cave-temple

106 Aihole. Durga temple of the late Gupta period; the design with the rounded apse is reminiscent of the Buddhist caitya-halls

107 Pattadakal. Virupaksha Temple, built by the Chalukya king Vikramatiya II, consecrated in 740. Shrine in the antechamber with the image of Nandi, Siva's bull

108 Lake in the jungle of the Western Ghats between the Malabar coast near Tellicherry and the high plateau of the Deccan

109 On the Backwaters of the Malabar coast amongst the coconut groves and the villages one frequently comes upon the Baroque façade of a church which goes back to the Portuguese period and is attended by the considerable Christian community in Kerala. The large fishing nets recall Chinese prototypes.

110 Trivandrum (Tiruvananantapuram), capital of Kerala, former capital of the princes of Travancore. Sri-Padmanabhaswami (Vishnu) Temple

111 Trichur. Gateway of the Great Temple with the roof-design that is characteristic of the architecture of the Malabar coast

112 Village on the Malabar coast; the houses with their palm-leaf roofs are reminiscent of Javanese domestic architecture.

113 Cochin. Pavilion in the temple pool

114 Boats on the canals on the Malabar coast; the cargo is usually coconuts, main product of this area

115 In Cochin harbour

116 Goa. Cathedral of St Katharina, 16th century, with a queue of worshippers on a feast-day. (Photo by Bernhard Moosbrugger from *Christian India* by F. A. Plattner)

117 Bijapur, Ibrahim Rauza. The mosque opposite the tomb (left) of Ibrahim II Adil Shah (1580–1626)

118 Bijapur. Sat-Manzili, *i.e.* seven-storied, today has five storeys, the highest of the palace buildings in the citadel

119 Bijapur. Jal Mandir, *i.e.* Water Pavilion, of the palace in the citadel

120 Bijapur. Jama Masjid (Great Mosque), begun under Ali I Adil Shah (1557–76), completed 1686. The Hall of Prayer

121 Bijapur. Gol Gumbaz, *i.e.* Round Dome, the tomb of Muhammad Adil Shah (1626–56), approximately 200 ft wide, diameter of the dome 122 ft

75

75-76 MYSORE

77

77-78 SRIRINGAPATNA

84

85

83-84 BELUR
85 SOMANATHPUR

86 HALEBID

87 SOMANATHPUR

89

89-90
SRAVANABELGOLA

91 SRIRANGAPATI

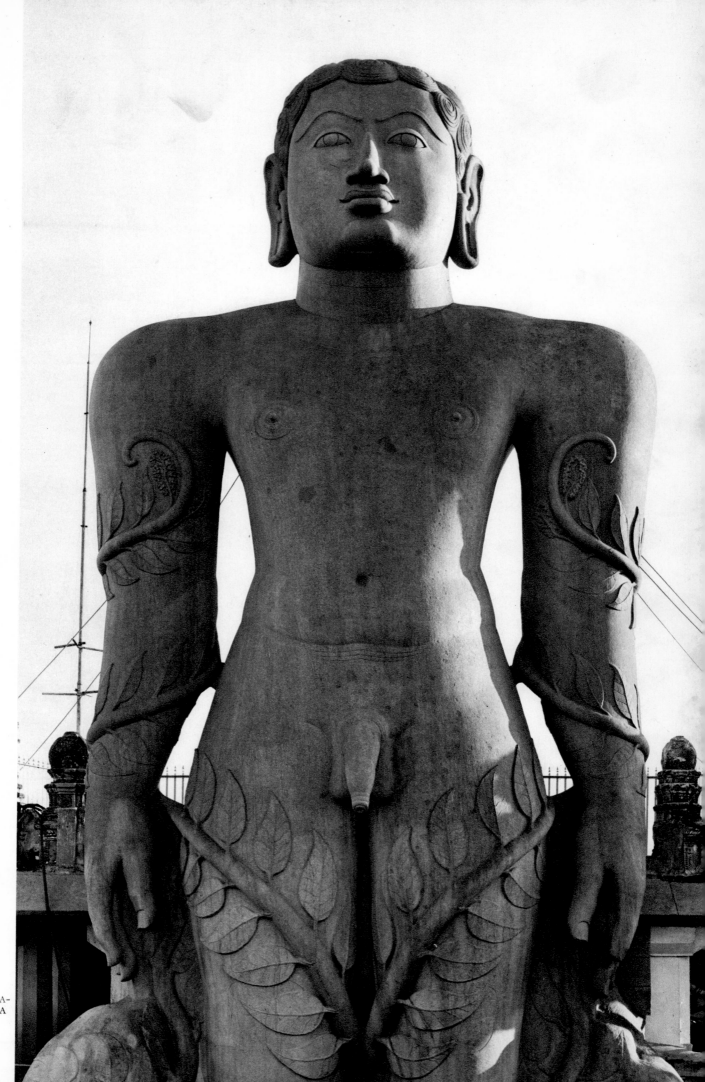

93

103

104

102–105 BADAMI

106 AIHOLE

107 PATTADAK.

110 TRIVANDRUM

111 TRICHUR

112 MALABAR

113 COCHIN

GOA

117

117-118 BIJAPUR

119–120 BIJAPUR

120

121 BIJAPUR, GOL GUMBAZ

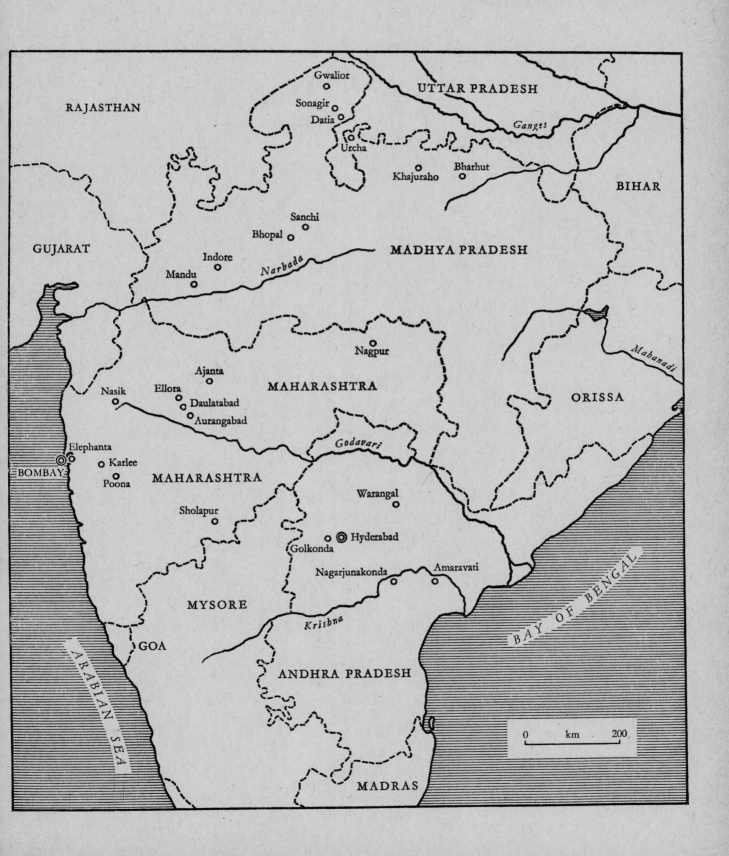

ANDHRA PRADESH
MAHARASHTRA
MADHYA PRADESH

ANDHRA PRADESH was formed from the northern part of the Madras Presidency in British India and the major part of the Nizam's possessions, until then by far the greatest of the principalities dependent on British India. This brought together the predominantly Telegu-speaking population, and Hyderabad, former residence of the Nizam, became their capital.

The old Andhra kingdom, which gave the new state its name, came into its own with the disappearance of the Maurya empire in the second century BC when the Andhras held a strong position between the Cholas, who were expanding southwards, and the Kalingas, who lived in the north and who had at one time been vassals of Asoka but had subsequently regained their independence; the Andhra kingdom stretched across the high plateau of the Deccan almost as far as Bombay, while the Kalingas inhabited the northern coastal strip of what is today Andhra Pradesh. But by the second century AD the prestige of the Andhras was clearly on the decline; their place was taken by the Pallavas in the south, the Chalukyas and Rashtrakutas in the west.

From the second to fourth centuries Mahayana Buddhism flourished on the lower reaches of the river Krishna at Amaravati, and at Nagarjunakonda, a place named after a Bodhisattva of Sinhalese origin. All that is still worth seeing of the buildings of that period has been placed in museums, and particular care has been taken recently to preserve the local collections. In the small museums at Amaravati and Nagarjunakonda, for example, there are admirable, richly-sculptured fragments of the great stupas, in which Buddhist art attained its greatest freedom and finesse, particularly in portraying the human figure. Parts of the Amaravati stupa, however, were removed as soon as they were discovered to the British Museum in London and the Indian Museum in Calcutta, and most of it to the museum in Madras.

The Kingdom of Golconda, which later became the Kingdom of the Nizam, was a product of the fighting between Bahmani and Warangal towards the end of the fifteenth century. Sultan Kuli Kutbul-Muk, a Turk in the service of the Bahmani ruler, turned the rocky hill of Golconda into a formidable fortress and founded a dynasty of his own, which left behind a splendid monument in the domed tombs at the foot of the mountain. The fifth ruler, Muhammad Kuli Kutb Shah, founded the

city of Hyderabad five miles to the west in 1589, a cit which was to become one of the most densely populate in India and the centre for all the crafts in the Deccan During his Deccan campaigns the Mogul empero Aurangzeb destroyed the Kingdom of Golconda in 168 but the fortress held out for another eight months and i the end was only subdued by a trick. Following th collapse of the Mogul Empire, the commander-in-chie of the emperor of Delhi, Ghaz-ud-din Khan Firoz Shah established his own dynasty, the head of which has sinc borne the title of Nizam. The tenth Nizam, who came t the throne in 1911 and who as a staunch Muslim rule over a preponderantly Hindu population, tried to retai the autonomy granted to him by the British, but Nehru' central government sent in troops to force his state to fi into the framework of the new India.

On 1 May 1960 the state of Bombay, which was mucl larger than the previous Bombay Presidency, wa broken up. The Gujarati-speaking northern part wa given its own administration, while the area in whicl Marathi was spoken, was called 'Maharashtra', a nam which has proud associations for the modern Indian. Th Marathas, who lived to the east of the Western Ghats, hac frequently given proof of their courage as mercenarie fighting for Muslim rulers, until in Shivaji (1627–80) the found a leader who made them a power in their own righ sufficiently strong even to defy the Grand Mogul o Delhi. Poets and preachers of the old Hindu doctrine such as Eknath and Tukaram, who were bold enough t oppose the 'Brahman priesthood', prepared the way fo Shivaji to become the legendary hero of a new Hindu state, which transcended all caste barriers, a hero who i still revered today by many patriots as the forerunner o an Indian nation.

After Shivaji's death the ageing Aurangzeb managed t reimpose the authority of the emperor of Delhi but only at great military cost. The city of Khadke, which had beer founded in 1610, was renamed Aurangabad and there ir the mausoleum which Aurangzeb built for his wife Rabila Daurani, is a sad reminder of the last of the great Moguls; for, had there been no Taj Mahal, this impressive monument might well have attracted considerable atten- tion, whereas it gives the impression of being merely a poor imitation of the splendid building in which

123 NAGARJUNAKONDA

Aurangzeb's dethroned father was laid to rest in Agra, and the unimposing tomb in Daulatabad of the tired and aged ruler is final proof that the golden age of Indo-Islamic history and art, which had dawned when Babur marched into Agra, was finally over.

But a new and third power had already gained a foothold in the port of Bombay and was to change the face of Maharashtra out of all recognition: the English brought trade and industry and opened the city to world commerce; Bombay became a power-house of the new India, in which the Marathas, far from being merely the victims of a foreign invasion, played and still play an active part.

The tourist who is interested in archaeology and whose first port of call in India is Bombay finds that the commercial glitter and bustle of this great city are eclipsed by the superabundance of works of art, which are hidden away in the famous cave-temples of Maharashtra. Within easy reach of the city with its teeming millions is the peaceful little island of Elephanta, where one can witness one of the most impressive demonstrations of Siva-worship. Although the rock whose shape gave the place its name fell to pieces during the last century and was reassembled in a park in Bombay, the largest of the caves, which were hollowed out of the rock between the sixth and eighth centuries, still has its sculptures intact. In the pillared hall stands the shrine with the lingam, and the reliefs which decorate the walls show Siva in various forms, all larger than life-size and surrounded by other worshipping godheads: as Ardhanariswara, who is half-man, half-woman, with his inseparable companion, the bull Nandi, then together with his wife Parvati celebrating marriage or sitting enthroned on Mount Kailasa, as a dancer shattering the world in the Tandava dance, as the fearful god of death Bhairava and as Lakulisa deep in Buddha-like meditation, but at his most gigantic as the three-headed Maheswara, a colossal bust the entire height of the wall facing the northern entrance. The building of the first cave-temples in India, at Gaya in the Bihar state, is generally attributed to the emperor Asoka. Until well into the tenth century more than a thousand such caves were hollowed out of the rock in various parts of India and in various architectural styles. In many of them the sculptural decoration, all of it wrought in the natural rock, is superbly planned and executed.

They fall into three main groups: the caves of Hinayana Buddhism date back to the period between the second century BC and the second century AD; the finest of the Mahayana caves with their sculptured figures, including the Buddha, belong to the fifth, sixth and seventh centuries. As in the earlier caves there are two main designs: the oblong caitya-hall, which opens out beyond a splendid front wall, is surrounded by pillars and serves as a place of prayer with the stupa situated in the apse at the rear—the finest example from the early period is the cave-temple of Karli—and the rooms of the 'vihara' or monastery, which sometimes has a verandah-like ante-chamber and has single cells or niches like small chapels round the central chamber. The most recent are the caves and rock-temples of the Hindus and Jains. Occasionally one finds displayed along the same rock-wall the sacred relics of several different periods and denominations. They were originally created as places of refuge for the monks, who spent the rainy season together in solitary communion with nature.

The Western Ghats, which lie behind Bombay, are particularly rich in caves and the specimens illustrated in this book are only a few chosen out of many scarcely less impressive others.

Two places where the profusion of monuments is almost overpowering are Ajanta and Ellora, both in the general region of Aurangabad.

In 1819 an English party hunting in the Indhyari mountains stumbled upon the caves of Ajanta at the entrance to a remote ravine, where they had remained forgotten ever since the collapse of Buddhism in south India in the seventh century.

Hiuen-tsang's account of it may sound rather fanciful today but it does convey the profound impression that was made on a visitor at a time when the days of the monastery were numbered. He writes:

On the eastern border of this country (Maharashtra) there is a great mountain with beetling crags and a chain of towering rocks and steep slopes. There, in a dark valley, a Sangharâma has been built. Its vast halls and deep aisles stretch over the face of the rocks. Storey upon storey looks down upon the river with the rocky crags as background. This monastery was built by the Arhat Achara, who came from western India ... The great hall of the monastery is about a hundred feet high. In the middle is a stone figure of Buddha, some seventy feet high. Over it rises a stone baldachin in seven stages and unsupported—it is said to be held thus in suspense by virtue of a vow made by Arhat . . . On the four sides of the vihara, on the stone walls, are painted various scenes from the life of the Tathagata in his life of preparation as Bodhisattva; these scenes are portrayed with the utmost precision and delicacy.

This series of twenty-six caves reflects the development from the modest viharas and caityas of Himayana Buddhism, the oldest of which date back as far as the second century BC, to the rich decorations of the Mahayana, when Buddha was no longer merely the great Teacher, who taught deliverance from suffering by means of knowledge, but was invested with a divine glory, surrounded by a host of Buddhas and Bodhisattvas who had gone before and come after him. The walls and ceilings of some Mahayana caves are lavishly painted with scenes from the Buddha legend, drawn in particular from the *Jatakas*, the books describing the Buddha's previous existences, which provided rich material for the inventive imagination of the painters, who were more readily inspired by worldly scenes than by depicting renunciation of the world. Despite repeated restoration work, in which outmoded methods were employed, and despite clumsy varnishing, these works of art are of inestimable value as the only major collection of early Indian painting.

The thirty-four caves at Ellora create, in part at least, quite a different impression: here we find in succession twelve Buddhist, seventeen Hindu and, a little apart, five Jain caves. Even when this place had ceased to be used regularly as a refuge by wandering ascetics, the popular fame of the temple persisted. In addition to the 'mandapas', the halls built into the rock, the Hindu architects and sculptors also hewed free-standing 'rathas' out of the rock face, working as always from above, detaching a rectangular block of stone from the mountainside and chiselling a temple out of it; they were also able to produce an exact imitation of masonry, similar to the 'rathas' of Mahabalipuram. The most famous of these rock-temples and a thing of prodigious beauty and achievement is the Kailasa—so-called after Siva's mountain. A courtyard with walls about a hundred feet high was hewn out of the basalt and in the centre a temple with

pillars, halls, steps, towers and a profusion of carved figures was hollowed out. On the open side a gateway shields it from the valley and the three walls of the courtyard are full of chapels and galleries, hewn out of the rock. An inscription which was put up when the work was completed bears the name of Krishna I, the second of the Rashtrakuta kings, who reigned c. 760–800 and made his dynasty the most powerful in the Deccan:

Krishnaraya instigated the building of a temple of wonderful design upon the mountain of Elapura. When the gods, floating through the air in their carriages, caught sight of it, they were overcome by astonishment and gave it much thought: 'This temple of Siva is sometimes unique, for no work of art can compare with it for beauty!' Even the master-builder, who constructed it, was struck with astonishment; at the thought that he might perform such a task again, his courage left him and he said: 'Wonderful? I know not myself how I succeeded in making this building!'

MADHYA PRADESH, the 'heart of India', produced in its long history a possibly even more bewildering array of empires and dynasties than other parts of India; among the ruling houses that shaped the country's history, successively, simultaneously or quite often in competition, were the Kshtrapas, the Satvahanas, the Nagas, the Vakatas, the Chalukyas, the imperial Guptas, the Rashtrakutas, the Pratiharas, the Yadavas, the Kacchawahas, the Haihayas, the Kalachuris, the Solankis, the Shailas, the Pamaras, the Chandels, the Gonds, the Tomaras and many more besides. In the eighteenth century the Marathas disputed the overlordship of the Mogul emperors of Delhi, till the British succeeded here too in imposing their authority. But even under their control a number of princely states of various sizes continued to enjoy a certain degree of self-government, until they were absorbed into the new republican system.

Here, midway between the plains of northern India and the high plateau of the Deccan, both the landscape and the monuments are extremely varied: jungles inhabited by wild animals and primitive tribes give way to fertile land or to mountains with great valleys, and everywhere man has left traces of his handwork and his religious beliefs, an inexhaustible reservoir of caves and fortresses, temples and palaces, which continue to lure the student of history and art from place to place long after he has visited and marvelled at the most famous of these monuments: the great Stupa of Sanchi from the pre-Christian era, the temples at Khajuraho built a thousand years later, and the mountain-fortress of Gwalior which belongs to more recent times.

After Buddha had reached Nirvana, his mortal remains were cremated and his followers distributed the sacred ashes among eight regions, in each of which a stupa was erected, not unlike the burial mounds of earlier civilizations. Later other stupas were built over other relics and the stupa became the most widespread Buddhist symbol throughout the whole of Asia. The hemispherical shape was chosen to symbolize the dome of heaven. It is surmounted by the 'yasti' or shaft, which carries the 'chatras', a series of carved panels that taper upwards to the roof—symbols of the divine host with Brahma at their head. A railing protects the shrine from the outside world, four gateways mark the four cardinal points, basing the design clearly on the design of the cosmos; this is the layout of the largest of the three stupas at Sanchi, which is reputed to have been built by the missionary-emperor Asoka. The stone railings, which are an imitation of earlier wooden railings, were decorated with reliefs in some of the most important early stupas—as, for example, at Amaravati and Nagarjunakonda. One of the oldest stone railings of this kind was at Bharhut in the northern part of what is today Madhya Pradesh; very little remains of it, unfortunately, for such fragments as were recovered were, for the most part, moved to the Indian Museum at Calcutta: the reliefs on the gateposts and on the architraves depict scenes from the Buddha legend, one of the most frequent showing the 'yakshis' reaching into the branches of a Sala tree: these were nature-spirits which also appear in the Mahabharata ('Who art thou who, bending the branch of the Kadamba tree, shines into the solitude of the hermit's cell, sparkling like flame in the night, tossed by the wind, oh thou of the shining countenance . . .'). Maya, the wife of Suddhodana, also held on to a branch of the same tree when she retired to the garden of Lumbi to give birth to Gautama, who became the Buddha. The reliefs of Bharhut, which seem archaic in their severity, are generally attributed to the Sunga period, the dynasty which followed the Mauryas in the second century BC but enjoyed a relatively short imperial life. It was the next period, that of the Satavahana or early Andhra art of central India in the first century BC that produced the four magnificently decorated doors of the great Stupa of Sanchi, which are among the real masterpieces of Asiatic art. On the beam of the east gate the yakshi suddenly appears at her boldest and most graceful, as if she were trying to hold up the cross-beams. In all these early works the Buddha himself, after attaining perfect Enlightenment, is never shown in human form but always symbolically; he is worshipped in the form of the stupa or as the Enlightened One in the Bo tree or as the Teacher in the empty throne.

Of quite a different character are the temples of Khajuraho, which date back to c. AD 1000, when the Chandela dynasty was flourishing in Bundelkhand. Hinduism had reached its peak and ruled unchallenged throughout India; worshippers of Vishnu and Siva vied with each other in building ever vaster temples and in filling them with a prodigious number of figures—more than eight hundred have been counted in the Kandariya Mahadeo. A group of Vishnu temples was built in Khajuraho and, when the rulers were converted to the cult of Siva, a second group was built, while the Jains, somewhat apart from the others, erected a third group, which except for the iconography, are outwardly indistinguishable from the 'Nagara' temples of the Hindus, tapering up to the tower over the shrine. The finest of these is the Kandariya Mahadeo from the reign of King Dhanga in the second half of the tenth century—in the central shrine stands the lingam of Siva and sculptured on the towering, beautifully symmetrical walls are those famous scenes in which fantasy lends to the divine a rich flavour of eroticism.

In the nineteen twenties a journey overland to these colossi in their setting of wild jungle was almost a form of exploration; today one can fly from Delhi to Khajuraho and back in one day—though it can only be a fleeting visit; visitors are received in a sort of park and the tourist office assures them that here is one of 'the world's topmost tourist attractions'.

The residences of former princely rulers with all their romantic associations belong to a more modern age. Mandu, the 'city of joy', was from 1405 the capital of

Hoshang Shah, whose father, as governor of Malwa, made himself independent of Delhi and founded the Ghor dynasty. The son of Hoshang Shah was murdered by one of his courtiers, who in his turn founded the Khilji dynasty and extended the city. The thirty-five mile long city wall and everything within it has long since been reclaimed by the jungle but even in their ruined state the palace buildings, which are scattered far and wide except for some that are grouped round a small lake, are among the most beautiful in India. In the present village lies the main mosque, which is in an excellent state of preservation, and close by is the domed tomb of Hoshang Shah, two of the finest examples of so-called Pathan or Afghan architecture. Even the emperor Jahangir, son of the great Akbar, was so impressed when he visited Mandu in 1616, that he recorded the event in his memoirs:

> The city was for a long time the residence of the kings of this land. Many buildings and souvenirs from the time of the old kings are still preserved. I rode out to inspect the royal buildings. First I visited the Jami Masjid, which was built by Sultan Hoshang Ghori. It is a very distinguished building, consisting entirely of hewn stone. Although it has been standing for 180 years, it looks as if it had been built today . . .

In Urcha (Orchha) and Datia one can see what imposing palaces were built even by the lesser Hindu princes under Muslim domination. But the most impressive of the princely residences in Madhya Pradesh is its northern outpost Gwalior, which is perched on a rocky mountain and was a formidable bulwark against the might of the sultans of Delhi and Agra. Legend has it than an ascetic named Gwalipa once lived on this mountain and with the aid of water from a pond cured the Rajput princeling

Suraj Sen of leprosy, as a result of which the first temple was built. In 1196 the fortress of Gwalior fell for the first time to the Muslims under Kutb-ud-din and it was taken by storm again in 1232 by Iltutmish (Altamsh), after the Rajput garrison had defended itself to the last man and their wives had committed 'johar' (suicide). Then in 1398, when Timur's invasion wrought havoc among the rulers of northern India, the Rajput leader Bir Singh Deo established himself in Gwalior and founded the Tomar dynasty, which from time to time paid tribute to the sultan of Delhi. From 1425 onwards, under the Tomar rulers, the great Jain figures appeared in a ravine in the mountain, and, although the first Mogul emperor, Babur, states tersely in his memoirs: 'I gave orders for these idols to be destroyed', these Tirthankaras in their characteristically rigid pose—there are several dozen of them, varying in size up to fifty-five feet in height—still remain, strangely alien to that landscape and yet concrete evidence that Mahavira's teaching continued under the protection of a few powerful patrons.

The greatest builder under the Tomars was Man Singh (1486–1516); the palaces built by him also influenced the architecture of the Mogul emperors, and indeed throughout the whole of India the western Asiatic, Islamic style and traditional Indian trends were reflected more and more in the architecture of the princes' palaces and in the conventions of their courts. Man Singh's successor fell in the battle of Panipat, which gave Babur control of northern India and also of Gwalior. In the eighteenth century, when the Mogul emperors gradually lost their empire, the Maratha leader Madho Rao Scindhia took possession of Gwalior (1784) and founded the last dynasty here, which proved a firm ally of the British Raj during the Mutiny of 1857, when the fortress was the scene of bitter fighting.

125 WARANGAL

122 Ajanta. Fresco in the Mahayana Buddhist Cave I, dating from *c.* AD 500. Detail from a palace scene

123 Nagarjunakonda. Vedika panel in a Buddhist stupa, depicting a stupa and the worship of Buddha. Andhra art of 2nd–4th centuries. Museum at Nagarjunakonda

124 Mandu. Jahaz Mahal, the 'Ship's Palace' between the two artificial lakes

125 Warangal. Part of a temple frieze showing a woman adorning herself. Black granite, *c.* 12th century. Archaeological Department, Government of Andhra Pradesh, Hyderabad

126 Gwalior. Palace of Man Singh (1486–1516), its walls decorated with coloured glazed tiles

127 Hyderabad. Char Minar, *i.e.* Four Towers, the Muslim emblem erected in 1591 by Mohammed Kuli Kutb Shah at a central cross-roads in the city

128 Golconda. The tombs of the Kutb Shahi kings (1507–1687) at the foot of the citadel

129 Golconda. Minaret of the Mosque belonging to the group of royal tombs

130, 131 Elephanta near Bombay, the great Siva Cave of the 8th–9th century. In the centre, opposite the main entrance, the 18 ft high, three-headed bust of Siva as Siva Mahadeva, with Aghora Bhairava or Siva the Destroyer crowned by a death's head on the left, and on the right the beautiful Uma (the figures are also interpreted as Siva's three manifestations: Brahma the Creator, Vishnu the Preserver and Rudra the Destroyer). In the niche to the left, separated by a column with a Dwarpal leaning on a dwarf, one of the ten large groups of sculpture with further manifestations of Siva: the god as Ardhana-risvara (*cf.* plate 31) leaning on the bull Nandi; to the right the dominating figure of Brahma on the lotus throne borne by five swans

132, 133 Nasik. From the group of 23 Pandu Lena caves of Hinayana Buddhism dating from the period of the Andhra kingdom, 1st century BC to 2nd century AD. The Caitya Cave (Cave 18), oldest of the group; the entrance decorated with sculptures of stupas (Dagobas); railings such as were erected around stupas, and windows. The interior represents the earliest and simplest form of Buddhist chapel or caitya-hall (*cf.* plates 136, 140, 143, 144)

134 From the group of nine 7th century Buddhist caves near Aurangabad, eight of which are Mahayana: the hall of the Vihara Cave 3, with two cells on either side, and the richly-ornamented columns of this late style

135, 136 The caitya-hall of Karli, 124 ft long and 45 ft high, is the largest of its kind; the 30 lateral columns have magnificent capitals and in the apse is the stupa or dagoba of the Hinayana, crowned by its ceremonial canopy but devoid of image. The cave goes back to 80 BC, the sculptures at the entrance (plate 135), where Buddha himself is depicted, belong to the later Mahayana period

137 Deogir, at one time capital of the Yadava dynasty, was given its present name Daulatabad, when the sultan of Delhi, Muhammad Tughlak, transferred the population of Delhi here in 1338. The fortification works in the Fort date back to the 13th century

138 The tomb near Aurangabad, which Aurangzeb built on the model of the Taj Mahal for his wife Rabia Daurani, who died in 1679

139 Pilgrims bathing at Nasik on the Godaveri, 'Ganges of the Deccan'

140 Ajanta. Façade of the caitya-hall of Cave 26; Mahayana Buddhist, from the latest period of the Ajanta caves, 6th–7th centuries

141 Ajanta. Cave 26. Detail of the frieze over the columns of the caitya-hall, with figures of Buddha and architectural designs

142 Ajanta. A specimen of sculptural ornamentation from the late Ajanta period

143 Ajanta. The caitya-hall in Cave 26

144 Ajanta. The caitya-hall in Cave 19; Mahayana, Gupta period, middle Ajanta period

145 Ajanta. Cave 12, from the Hinayana group dating back to pre-Christian times. Vihara hall with entrances to monks' cells

146 Ellora. The Kailasa Temple from the reign of the Rashtrakuta king Dantidurga, 725–55

147 Ellora. Cave 10, Viswakarma or Carpenters' Cave, with a verandah which forms the entrance to the caitya-hall; Mahayana Buddhist, after 700

148 Ellora. Cave 29 (Hindu), Sita-ki-Nahani; *c.* 700. Siva as Virabhadra

149 Ellora. Cave 29. Niche by the entrance (right): Siva

and Parvati enthroned on Kailasi, which is borne aloft by Ravana

150 Ellora. Cave 39. Niche on the east side of the south wing; the marriage of Siva and Parvati

151 Ellora, Cave 31. Jain sculptures in the uncompleted cave of Chhota Kailasa

152 Ellora. Cave 31. The Avatara (Hindu) Hall in the upper storey with Siva's bull, Nandi

153 Khajuraho. The Kandarya Mahadeo Temple from the south-west (*cf.* plate 8)

154 Khajuraho, Kandarya Mahadeo Temple; ceiling of the antechamber

155 Khajuraho, Kandarya Mahadeo Temple. Corridor surrounding the central shrine

156 Khajuraho, Kandarya Mahadeo Temple. The Shrine with the lingam in place of the scared image

157 Mandu. View across the grounds of the palace and the bathing-quarters at the north end of the Munja Tank looking towards Jahaz Mahal

158 Mandu. Jama Masjid (the Great Mosque), started under Hoshang Shah and completed in 1454 under Mahmud Khilji I

159 Mandu. The marble tomb of Alif Khan Hoshang Shah Ghori (1406–35)

160 Bhopal. Taj-ul-masajid, designed by Shah Jahan Begam, who acted as Nawab until 1901; one of the largest mosques in India

161 Amaravati. Medallion from the stone railing of a stupa showing Rabula being led before his father, the Buddha; the latter is represented symbolically by the throne with the footprints before it and above it a fiery pillar with the Triratna sign. Andhra style, *c.* 2nd century AD. Amaravati Museum

162 Sanchi. The great stupa founded by Asoka, extended during the early Andhra period (1st century BC), when the four gates of the stone railing were added. View from the south with the south gate

163 Sanchi. Right-hand pillar of the north gate of the great stupa. Worship of the Buddha symbolized by the Bodhi tree. In the lower panel, a monkey offers the Buddha honey

164 Sanchi. West gate seen from the east. Worship of the Buddha is symbolized by the Wheel of the Law and the stupa. On the cross-beam of the architrave scenes showing the various princes who quarrelled over the recovery of the relics after Buddha's entry into paranirvana

165 Sanchi. The great stupa seen from the south-east; on the left the columns of a caitya-hall which goes back to the Sunga period and renewed in the 7th century; in the foreground the foundations of one of the other stupas which covered the plateau

166 Sanchi. Relief on the north gate of the great stupa. Emperor Asoka (or King Bimbasara of Magadha or King Prasenajit of Sravast), shaded by a ceremonial umbrella, pays homage to the Buddha, who is represented by the Bodhi tree

167 Figure of a warrior from the stone railing of the stupa of Bharhut, Sunga period (*c.* 1st century BC). Indian Museum, Calcutta

168, 169 Nagarjunakonda. Ayaka frieze with mythological scenes from a stupa. Light green limestone, Andhra art, *c.* 3rd century AD. Nagarjunakonda Museum

170 Sonagir, one of the isolated sacred mountains of the Jains, on which numerous temples have been built in recent centuries

171 Urcha (Orchha). The Chaturbhuy Temple belonging to the prince's residence of the 17th century

172 Datia, capital of a former principality. The palace built by Bir Singh Deo in the 17th century

173 Urcha. The palace of Bir Singh Deo; 17th century

174 Gwalior. At the foot of the citadel lies the tomb of Muhammad Ghau, a Muslim of the 16th century who was revered as a saint

175 Gwalior. Room in Man Singh's palace (1486–1516)

176 Gwalior. The Temple of Telika Mandir, a shrine of Vishnu which presumably goes back to the 9th century but has been a shrine of Siva since the 15th century

177 Gwalior. One of the monumental Jain figures on the mountainside

127 HYDERABAD

128 GOLKONDA

129 GOLKONDA

130–131 ELEPHANTA

132–133 NASIK   133

134 AURANGABAD

137 DAULATABAD

138 AURANGABAD

139 NASIK
140 AJANTA

143

141–143 AJANTA

144

153 KHAJURAHO

151–152 ELLORA

157-158 MANDU

158

159 MANDU

160 BHOPAL

163

164

165

68

170 SONAGIR

171 URCHA

172 DATIA

173 URCHA

174–176 GWALIOR

175

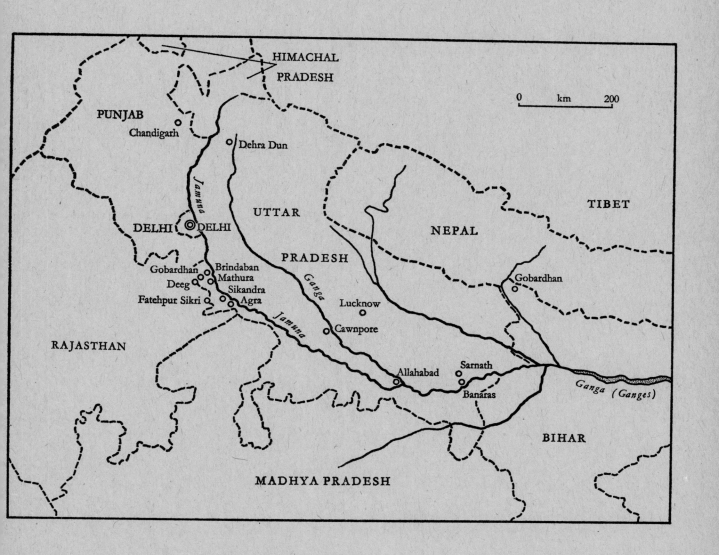

DELHI
UTTAR PRADESH

In the Manava Dharma Sastra, which are ascribed to Manu, the legendary legislator of the Indo-Aryans, the land of Aryavarta is described as stretching from ocean to ocean between the Himalayas and the Vindhya mountains, and the area known today as Uttar Pradesh, which took its initial letters from the former United Provinces, corresponds, together with the federal territory of Delhi, roughly to the old Madyadesa, the middle land.

In the ancient hymns, textbooks and epic tales of Hinduism that period is very much alive, when the Indo-Aryan herdsmen took possession of the country, mingled with the Dravidians and established their first kingdoms. In the uninhibited creation of religious legends the priests and poets were masters; the extent to which they drew upon real events was something that did not interest the Hindus. It was possible, if not probable, that the father of all, Manu, the hero, Rama, and the mischievous cow-herd Krishna had been modelled on real men. But we know that there was hardly a human passion that was unfamiliar to this volatile people or unworthy of a god. They were capable of loyalty and treachery, could be as cruel as they could be magnanimous, both vindictive and forgiving, they flung themselves into battle and between-times listened spellbound to words of profound wisdom. There was no earthly joy too mean for them and they had an insatiable appetite for love. But they also had a rigid social system which kept the family, the caste and the village community together and enabled them to survive the struggles and follies of the potentates.

When Krishna was born at Mathura at the end of the third era, his uncle, King Kamsa, sought to take his life, as it had been predicted to the king that one of his sister's children would assassinate him. But like Moses and Jesus the boy succeeded in a miraculous way in foiling the evil king's plans. Named Krishna ('the black one') because of his blue-black complexion, he grew up with foster-parents as a cow-herd and before long his comrades were amazed not only by his miracles but also by his mischievous pranks. The district of Gobardhan and Brindaban is the scene of many of the colourful stories about him, which provided material for poets, sculptors and painters for many centuries; Krishna lifting Mount Gobardhan in order to protect the herdsmen from the torrent of rain poured down by a furious Indra, Krishna stealing the shepherdesses' clothes as they bathed and indulging in countless amorous adventures, but above a[l] Krishna courting the lovely Radha. Krishna's cows, hi[s] dance and his flute-playing. After he had wandered far an[d] wide throughout the land, even as far as Gujarat and ha[d] sired thousands of sons, he finally died, like Achilles, whe[n] a hunter, mistaking him for a gazelle in the woods, sho[t] an arrow into the only vulnerable part of his body, th[e] heel. He thereupon resumed his divine form as Vishnu.

In the *Mahabharata* Krishna is also the fount of divin[e] wisdom, who explains to Arjuna before the great battl[e] the meaning of action that is devoid of all earthly purpos[e] but motivated solely by pure love of God, action whic[h] can be as appropriate to the warrior as to the ascetic:

Who in his deeds thinks only of me in life,
loves me above all else, is entirely dedicated to me,
Who hates no one and who may cling to no thing,
he, oh son of Pandu, will one day reach me.

From this legendary period only the literature remain[s]. The Temples of Mathura (Muttra), Brindaban an[d] Gobardhan are more recent in origin and their ornamen[-] tation already betrays a kinship with Muslim building[s]. Mathura is a busy, modern town, but the Museu[m] (founded in 1933) gives ample evidence of the importanc[e] attached to this place in the early Buddhist and late[r] periods; regular discoveries have been made of treasure[s] from the golden age of sculpture between the times of th[e] Mauryan and the Gupta empires.

Not far from modern Delhi lay Hastinapura, whe[re] Bharata had founded the kingdom of Bharata Varsha i[n] prehistoric times. For eighteen days the battle rage[d] between his successors, the five Pandava brothers and th[e] Kauravas, an event which is described in the *Mahabhara[ta]* and for which the authors presumably drew on th[e] traditional accounts of the struggle of the Aryans, wh[o] had poured into the country in waves, to carve it up int[o] states. Yudhishthira, the eldest of the five victoriou[s] Pandavas, celebrated the great horse-sacrifice (asvamedha[)] with which a king announced to heaven and to mankin[d] his claim to the imperial rank of a world ruler.

The next great battle which decided the fate of centr[al] India was fought in the full glare of history and wa[s] faithfully recorded by the first chronicles to emerge i[n] India since the Chinese pilgrims. In the twelfth centur[y] when Indraprashtra, the modern Delhi, was ruled by th[e]

179

180

179 DELHI,
MAUSOLEUM
TUGHLAQ S

180 DELHI,
MAUSOLEUM
FIROZ SHAH

Rajput Prithvi Raj, the Islamic invasion from the west was becoming increasingly threatening. The Arabs had already established themselves in Sind on the lower Indus in the eighth century. Since 1001 Mahmud of Ghazni had been making repeated raids from his base in Afghanistan and had even captured the holy city of Mathura. In 1173 the princes of Ghor took over Ghazni and Muhammad of Ghor, the younger brother of King Ghyas-ud-din, conquered the parts of western India which had been occupied by other Muslim princes, and in the winter of 1190–91 he led his army against the kingdom of Indra-prashtra. At Tarain, where Mahmud of Ghazni had defeated a Hindu army 180 years earlier, Prithvi Raj confronted the invader with a mighty army. The Indian centre stood firm against the furious cavalry attacks and Muhammad himself, who in the thick of battle had caught sight of the raja's brother, Govind Raj, shattered his teeth with a blow of his lance but was himself seriously wounded in the arm and fled the field just in time to save his life. But by the following year Muhammad had assembled a fresh army and another battle was fought at Tarain. The Muslim leader on this occasion met superior numbers with superior tactics. For hours he launched attack after attack on the opposing wings till the Hindu army was in such a state of confusion that the final attack by twelve thousand picked cavalry in the centre came as a complete surprise and sealed the raja's fate: Prithvi dismounted from his elephant and took to flight on horseback but was caught and killed at the Sarasvati river. Early in 1193, Indraprashtra, later renamed Delhi, was also occupied. Muhammad appointed his outstanding general, Kutb-ud-din Aibak, whom he had originally acquired as a slave, viceroy of the conquered territory. In 1206 while Muhammad was camping on the banks of the Indus, two Indians slipped into his tent during the siesta and murdered him. Kutb-ud-din, who had served his master faithfully, thereupon proclaimed himself sultan of Delhi: he was the first of the 'Slave Kings', the first of a long succession of rulers who changed the face of ancient Madhyadesa, the middle land, and of India as a whole. From then on in Hindustan, as Aryavarta came to be called, Delhi was the leading capital, the only place whose occupant could claim the imperial title, even if the sultan's actual power did not always extend beyond the modern territory of the federal capital.

The Islamic usurpers, who set up their kingdoms in India—coming from the south, we have already found traces of them in Golconda, Bijapur, Aurangabad and Mandu—brought not only their religion with them but also their own highly developed culture. It was the second major invasion of India following the Aryan incursion. But, while the religion and civilization of the people of the Vedas spread throughout India and in some mysterious way mingled with the existing culture of the Dravidians, the Islamic invasion came to a halt midway, and the two cultures, which had been in a state of conflict ever since the Islamic-Indian rule became established in the thirteenth century, have remained irreconcilable to the present day. Although they influenced one another to a considerable extent, although there was tolerance on both sides—and despite the periods of bloody persecution it was the general rule—although there was inter-marriage, with the princes themselves setting the example, the gulf between Mohammed's commandments and the teachings of the Brahmans was never bridged. Not a few states remained under the rule of the rajas side by side with Muslim states, large and small. For the most part the population, even those living under Islamic rulers, remained true to their Hindu faith, but the old social order was no longer supreme; the power of the new reigning princes with their picked troops recruited from their own tribesmen and with the converted, who usually came from the lowest castes and to whom Islam offered equal rights for all believers, came to represent a vital factor in India's national life.

The Muslim usurpers in India were not only masters in the art of war, they were also, for the most part, highly cultivated people and loved to surround themselves with splendid buildings; together with their religious and legal scholars they brought poets, historiographers and architects, and the cultural heritage they introduced from the Near East blossomed in the soil of ancient Aryavarta into something that was no less Indian than Islamic.

The fact that most Muslim architects shared the predilection of the Indian temple and palace builders for rich decoration meant that the *genius loci* was given free play; the layout of the temple-courts with their arcades and niches was also reflected in the courtyards of the mosques. The richly ornamented pillars of the Hindu temples were adopted without a qualm for the prayer-halls of the mosques and even such sacred ancient monuments as the famous iron column of Lal Kot were erected to lend authenticity to the 'Triumph of Islam'—as Kutb-ud-din called his first great mosque in Delhi—on Indian soil. While any form of imagery is forbidden in Muslim buildings—strictly speaking, not even plants can be depicted—such was the imagination of the decorators that they produced an infinite variety of abstract ornaments, in which Tughra characters were sometimes interwoven with quotations from the Koran and memorial inscriptions. The basic design characterizing Muslim buildings came to predominate and the highly ornate tower soaring above the sacred images of the Hindus gave way to the ground-plan, to design in space, to simple clarity. The fifty feet high central vault in the Quwwat-ul-Islam mosque (Triumph of Islam) marked the introduction of the vault, the enormous Kutb Minar, erected by the same builders, turned the minaret into a victory column, and in the dome there are countless variations on the same theme of victory. India was not the only country to which the building of mausoleums came as something quite new—unless one chooses to regard them as merely a continuation of the circular design of the stupa. Mohammed himself forbade any such glorification of the dead. The pharaohs and the Chinese emperors had built magnificent tombs—for them the burial-place of a ruler was the expression of an inviolate and almighty power linking the earth with the cosmos. The sultans of Delhi, however, and later the rulers of Golconda, Bijapur, Ahmadabad and other princely capitals, erected their domed mausoleums on alien soil as evidence that history had been made in a world that had previously been devoid of history.

One reads of the seven cities of old Delhi, and scattered over some forty square miles lie the ruins of the fortified capitals which various dynasties built here, where the Jumna flows down from the highlands of the Punjab into the plains of Hindustan. A visitor from Damascus, Shahab-ud-din Abdul Abbas Ahmad, wrote of Delhi in the first half of the fourteenth century:

Delhi consists of an accumulation of twenty-one cities. The houses are built of stone and tile, the roofs of wood. The stone in the floors is as white as marble; in the sultan's palace they are of marble. The newer houses, however, are built in a different style. Delhi is surrounded on three sides by gardens, while the western side is bounded by mountains. There are a thousand schools, seventy hospitals, two thousand chapels and hermitages, large monasteries, wide open courtyards and many baths.

And Ibn Batuta referred to Delhi as 'actually one of th largest cities in the universe'.

A table of dates may perhaps help to pinpoint the variou builders and dynasties, who in more or less natura succession made themselves masters of old Delhi:*

1193–1210

Kutb-ud-din Aibak occupies Delhi and in 1206 assume the title of sultan. He builds at Lal Kot the Quwwat-ul Islam mosque and starts the construction of the grea tower of prayer and victory, Kutb Minar.

1211–1236

Out of the confusion following Kutb-ud-din's death th son-in-law of the first sultan, Iltutmish (also called Altamsh) emerges, likewise a former slave. The caliph o Baghdad formally acknowledges his title of 'Sultan o India' and he is reputed to have been a strong and jus ruler and a strict Muslim. The great mosque is extended the construction of the Kutb Minar continued. The tomb which adjoins the mosque is believed to be his and therefore ranks as the oldest royal tomb in Delhi. Hi successors rule until 1266; they are followed by Balba (1266–90), who in his turn was succeeded by the Khilj dynasty (until 1320).

1296–1316

Ala-ud-din Muhammad removes his uncle Jalal-ud-din Firuz by base treachery. He adds a third courtyard to the great mosque of Lal Kot and begins the construction of a tower which is to surpass even the Kutb Minar.

1320–1325

Ghyas-ud-din Tughlak, founder of the Tughlak dynasty (until 1413), acquires the reputation during his short reign of being one of the most capable rulers of Delhi. He builds Delhi's 'third city', the fortress of Tughlakabad, and with it his own domed mausoleum, which is distinguished by its severe lines.

* *A more detailed account, with illustrations, can be found in our book on Delhi, Agra and Fatehpur Sikri (1964).*

1325–1351

Muhammad Shah, who succeeds his father, is, according to Ibn Batuta, 'man who above all likes giving presents and shedding blood'. His deeds of generosity and courage have become as well known as his cruel acts of violence. Infuriated by the petitions reproaching him with his misdeeds, he banishes the entire population of Delhi to Daulatabad and later repopulates the city with people from other provinces.

1351–1388

Firoz Shah, who succeeds his cousin, is regarded as a just ruler; he is one of the great builders of Delhi; he constructs, among others, the palaces and mosques of Firozabad and the religious school of Hauz-i-Khas, where his tomb also stands, and at the same time he preserves older buildings.

1398

Timur, emir of Samarkand, invades India on the pretext that the Muslim rulers have shown less religious zeal than the Hindus. In December Delhi is mercilessly looted. After Timur's withdrawal the last of the Tughlak kings manages to resume his throne and in 1412 he dies, the last of his dynasty. Under the subsequent Saiyid rulers Delhi reaches the nadir of its power.

1451

Bahlol Lodi takes over from the last of the Saiyids and founds the Lodi dynasty, which rules until 1526. The domed tombs of the three Lodi kings and other notable personalities, together with their mosques, are fine examples of the Pathan style.

1502

Sikandar Lodi transfers his capital from Delhi lower down the Jumna to Agra, which until then has been virtually unknown but seems to him to be strategically better placed, particularly with an attack on Gwalior in view.

1526

Ibrahim Lodi suffers a crushing defeat by Babur, founder of the Mogul dynasty, at the battle of Panipat.

Babur, who was descended from two of the greatest conquerors in history, Timur and Genghis Khan, founded the dynasty which was to have the longest and most brilliant period of rule, that of the Moguls. Throughout six generations of great emperors the supreme title passed from father to son, although within the family the impatience of the sons and rivalry among the brothers gave rise to constant struggles for power.

Babur, who had grown up in an atmosphere of suspicion and hostility, was not merely a daring general; his memoirs reveal him as a man of many interests and a colourful personality with a frankness that was both novel and engaging. Of his ambitions as a conqueror he writes:

> Ever since I had conquered the land of Kabul, which occurred in the year AH 910 (AD 1504), it had always been my aim to subdue Hindustan, and in the course of seven or eight years I invaded it five times at the head of an army. The fifth time Almighty God in His goodness and mercy permitted me to defeat an enemy as powerful as Sultan Ibrahim (Lodi) and made me master of the great Kingdom of Hindustan.

After his victory Babur inspected the monuments of earlier kings in Delhi, gave instructions that the 'kutba' (sermon) should be read in his name in the main mosque during the Friday prayers and that money should be distributed to the fakirs and beggars; but then he moved on without delay to Agra.

> After my arrival in Agra, I crossed the Jumna and looked around for a suitable piece of land to lay out a garden. It always seems to me that Hindustan lacks nothing so much as canals, so I had resolved that, wherever I finally settled, I would construct water-wheels, produce artificial streams and lay out a beautiful park. But everything I saw was so ugly that I returned across the river quite disgusted . . . But as I could find no more favourable spot than Agra, I was finally compelled to make the best of what was there . . . Three things in Hindustan caused us inconvenience: heat, strong winds and dust. Baths were the means whereby all three hardships could be overcome simultaneously.

Babur died in 1530 at the early age of forty-eight and nothing remains of what he built. His son Humayun, on the other hand, had little time to build, for this well-meaning man was pursued by misfortune, and the chances that the Mogul dynasty would survive seemed fairly remote until the Afghan Sher Shah, who had made himself master of Bihar and was a much more capable ruler, seized the throne of Delhi in 1539. Sher Shah once remarked, pointing to his white beard, that supreme power had only come to him at the time of the evening prayer. He employed the six years still left to him more fully than any ruler before him. He found time not merely to conduct campaigns and to build up a highly disciplined army but also to introduce a new and efficient taxation system, land-surveys and a book-keeping system in both Persian and Hindi; he established the rule of law and stamped out corruption, built major highways bordered by fruit trees and equipped with caravanserais at regular intervals, where Muslims and Hindus were provided with separate accommodation; and wherever the authority of his police extended, people were secure against robbery. Sher Shah was also a great builder: under him India's Pathan architecture reached its zenith; in Delhi he built the gigantic fortress-wall of Purana Qila (i.e. old city) with its ceremonial gateway and one of the most beautiful mosques in the country, noble and generous in design, delicate and rich in decorative detail. It was said of his workmen: 'They began their buildings like giants and finished them like goldsmiths.'

Humayun, who had taken temporary refuge with the Shah of Persia, survived Sher Shah's son and successor, Islam Shah, and succeeded in reoccupying Delhi in 1555. He took up residence in Purana Qila but died only a few months later as a result of a fall on the polished stairs of his library. No visitor to Delhi should neglect to visit his tomb, for his widow, Hamida Begum, in commissioning the architect Miruk Ghiya to build it, enabled him to produce his greatest masterpiece. It took nine years to build. In the centre of the garden, which is surrounded by walls and gateways, stands the vast substructure of the mausoleum surmounted by the dome of the tomb itself with its double cupola and the marked protuberance of the outer white marble shell, which is Persian in origin and is so characteristic of Mogul cupolas.

Akbar succeeded his father Humayun at the age of thirteen and when he was eighteen dismissed his tutor and acting regent. He inherited the boundless energy of his grandfather Babur. His son Jahangir, whose relations with his father were far from happy, described him as follows:

> Although he could neither read nor write, he had so cultivated his speech by regular intercourse with scholars and poets that no one would have taken him for an uneducated man. He had a remarkably sound

feeling for the finer points of poetry and prose . . . His demeanour distinguished him from other men and his countenance radiated a godlike dignity.

Akbar chose Agra as his capital. Amongst the many military and administrative tasks he set himself to make his empire secure, he devoted himself with particular enthusiasm to building and to religion. From 1562 to 1579 he made a yearly pilgrimage to Ajmer and on several occasions made the long journey on foot. Whenever he heard of some wise man who had became famous, he sought him out and tried to learn the secret of his wisdom. Such was his passionate interest in other religions—even Jesuits were given a friendly reception at his court—that he finally neglected the faith of his forefathers and became increasingly convinced that he himself was an instrument of God for the establishment of a universal religion which would unite all his subjects.

Of the rebuilding of Agra, Akbar's son wrote:

> An old fort stood there; it had already been demolished by my father before I was born and he had it rebuilt in hewn red stones, the like of which travellers, who had travelled the world, had never seen. Building continued for 16 or 17 years.

And Akbar's court chronicler Abul Fazl wrote of the work which began in 1569: 'Five hundred buildings of stone in the beautiful style of Bengal and Gujarat were built with the collaboration of the most experienced artists.' Amongst the models were the palaces of the Hindu princes, for example in nearby Gwalior. Akbar's grandson, Shahjahan, who had ambitious plans of his own, left only the southern wing standing, which is known as Jahangiri Mahal; it was presumably used as the heir to the throne's residence and is an impressive example of Akbar's later style, the sandstone blocks covered with an endless variety of abstract patterns.

But Akbar also built himself a new capital, which was barely completed when it was abandoned again and is today a vast museum of architectural masterpieces. While the emperor was visiting Sheikh Salim Chishti in his village, Sikri, some twenty miles from Agra, the devout hermit prophesied that the emperor would have the heir he had so long desired. When shortly afterwards Akbar's Hindu wife, a daughter of the Rajput prince of Amber, became pregnant, she had to retire to the sheikh's humble hermitage to await the birth of her child. And on 30

August 1569 Prince Salim was born, and later, when he became the Emperor Jahangir, he wrote:

My revered father, who saw in the village of Sikri, where I was born, a place of good omen for himself, transferred his capital there and in the course of fifteen or sixteen years the hills and steppes, home of many wild animals, were transformed into a splendid city with many gardens, elegant palaces and pavilions and a large number of other attractive houses. After the conquest of Gujarat (1573) the place was named Fatehpur (properly called Fathabad), which means City of Victory.

The local quarries provided beautiful red sandstone, and the emperor, who to begin with took up residence with the sheikh, urged on the builders and also supervised the construction of a nearby water-reservoir. From 1572 onwards one building after the other was completed, including a particularly fine house for Raja Birbal, the most influential Hindu at the court, and the ruler and his family were able to exchange the palace at Agra, which, according to the superstitious, was inhabited by evil spirits, for the new residence. One of its most unusual features, which was presumably the emperor's own idea, is the audience-chamber, which is dominated by a central column that opens out at the top like a flower. After his victory at Gujarat, Akbar added the huge victory gate Buland Darwaza to the great mosque, where he himself proclaimed his new religion from the pulpit. When Sheikh Salim Chishti died in 1572, he was buried in a splendid white marble tomb in the courtyard of the mosque.

But the climate of Fatehpur Sikri proved to be unhealthy. The dam of the reservoir broke and no one showed any interest in restoring it. In 1585 the emperor moved to the Punjab and only paid one more fleeting visit to his new city. The population scattered and during Akbar's last years the court returned to Agra.

Jahangir, who ruled from 1605 to 1627, is overshadowed by his great father. He spared neither effort nor money to complete Akbar's tomb at Sikandra near Agra, an unusual, pyramid-shaped building in a magnificent setting, which is entered by way of a gate surrounded by minarets. On the opposite bank of the Jumna, facing Agra, stands the tomb—built during the same period—of his father-in-law and lifelong counsellor, the Persian nobleman Itimat-ud-daula: although it cannot compete with the grandiose setting of the imperial tomb, the rich marble trellis-work and the delicate colours of the inlaid stones are among the finest examples of Mogul art.

Jahangir did not feel at home either in Agra or in Delhi and preferred Lahore in what is today western Pakistan, where he was eventually buried. In later years he left the conduct of state affairs more and more to his much more forceful Persian wife Nur Mahal, with the result that historians have branded him as a weak ruler; but never were poets and painters made so welcome at the court of the Grand Mogul as under Jahangir and no court has ever produced more beautiful miniatures.

His successor, Shah Jahan, was thirty-six when he ascended the throne. As Prince Khurram he had staged more than one bloody revolt against his father and owed his life solely to his father's mercy. He had tricked his elder brother out of the succession and arranged for his nephew, who had been proclaimed emperor, to be strangled. The imperial house had by now lost almost all trace of the foreign conquerors. Under the tolerant Akbar mixed marriages with the families of native princes had become quite customary, and Shah Jahan through his father's mother and his own mother was three-quarters descended from Hindu princes of Rajputana.

Shah Jahan has become famous as being the greatest of India's imperial builders. Building was a passion with him, which possessed him more completely than any of his predecessors, and during the long period of peace which followed on the Deccan wars in the early part of his reign he was able to indulge his obsession almost without bounds. In addition to the local red sandstone, which had been used for so many buildings before his time, white marble now came into its own, and the marble quarries of Makrana in Rajputana were exploited as never before. An army of skilled stonemasons worked on the slabs, chiselling delicate flower-patterns in bas-relief. Precious coloured stones were collected and set painstakingly (*pietra dura*) in the marble surfaces.

A court chronicler described how Shah Jahan devoted part of his day to his building projects:

The Emperor spends part of his time inspecting the work of such excellent craftsmen as the stone-cutter and the enameller. The overseers of the royal buildings, with the wondrously gifted masters of the art to advise them, submit their plans to His Majesty's critical eye. The royal mind, sublime as the sun, devotes its entire attention to the lofty buildings and strong walls, which, in accordance with the popular saying 'truly our buildings speak for us', will for a long time to come proclaim with silent tongue their master's magnanimity and his sublime happiness and will continue in the distant future to bear witness to his love af beauty and purity. Most of the buildings he designs himself. After the most careful consideration he makes alterations in the plans worked out by the skilled architects and poses expert questions. On the approved plans Yamin-ud-daulah Asaf Khan, this strong pillar of the Empire and right arm of the Monarch, writes the explanatory sacred (imperial) instructions for the master-builder and overseers to carry out.

Shah Jahan's overriding ambition was to convert the Palace of Agra, where three years before ascending the throne he had figured as a rebel and plunderer, into one of the most magnificent royal residences in the world. His aim was not to build a mere pompous façade like that of the Sun King at Versailles or of his imitators; he was never greatly interested in the monumental for its own sake and, when he was, then it was as a deliberate contrast. Having walked through the great fortress-gate and passed the guards, one found oneself in the elegant and intimate atmosphere of open audience-chambers, gardens, pavilions, baths and living-rooms. And anyone fortunate enough to visit this museum of architecture today with its polished marble and its vast empty spaces must see with his mind's eye these halls and gardens throbbing with life and colour, as European travellers like Tavernier and Bernier so graphically described them or as contemporary painters portrayed them in such magical detail in their miniatures, the backcloth of carpets and silverware, the procession of imperial notables, the groups of musicians, the parade of horses, elephants and other animals in the courtyards, the splashing of the fountains, the graceful inhabitants of the harem.

After barely three years on the throne the emperor lost the most beloved of his wives, Mumtaz Mahal, a niece of his father's wife, Nur Mahal, and to assuage his grief he resolved to build a tomb in her honour, which would surpass in beauty anything that had ever been built before. And it is certainly true to say that no building has captivated the minds of people the world over as this memorial of love has done; even those who have barely heard of Agra and the Grand Mogul and who have no interest whatsoever in the mysteries of architecture are nevertheless aware of the glory of the Taj Mahal. According to Tavernier, twenty thousand men worked for twenty-two years on the construction. The scaffolding cost as much as the building itself, as timber was not available and stone had to be used instead. The design, in which the emperor himself undoubtedly took an active and continuous interest, embraced an entire complex of buildings and gardens: from the palace-like gateway, mainly of sandstone, the visitor has an uninterrupted view of the white domed building rising behind a rectangular pool in the midst of the vast garden, a view which has been captured in countless pictures and which is also included in this book as representing what the architect clearly intended to be our first sight of the building. As one approaches it, one is immediately struck by the delicate filigree work of the inscriptions, floral decorations and abstract designs, which does not detract, however, from the clear lines of the architecture. The tomb is flanked on either side by an imposing mosque and a similar building which are in perfect symmetry and built of the same red sandstone as the main gateway; they serve to bring out with startling effect the white pearly sheen and magnificent proportions of the main building as it soars above its marble base.

In the eleventh year of his reign and before the building was completed, Shah Jahan decided to transfer his capital from Agra to Delhi and to build a new residence amongst the ancient monuments of the old city. He had a detailed survey made to ascertain whether the climate was suitable and whether a fortress could be built, and over the next ten years the city with the Red Fort was built on the Jumna, which was called Shahjahanabad but gradually became known as Delhi and as such has remained to this day a city of gay bazaars and of crafstmen, a focal point for merchants and a favourite port of call for travellers. Masons and artisans were drawn from all over the empire, and the transportation of stone from the quarries at Agra assumed such proportions that traders complained about interference with normal commercial traffic.

A wall six miles long with seven gates forms the outer perimeter and the central axis is the seventy feet wide street of the silversmiths, Chandni Chauk, which runs from the entrance to the fort past the Sikh temple Sisganj Gurdwara, a later construction, to the Fatehpuri Mosque. In the maze of narrow streets one relic of earlier times remains, the sober Kalam Masjid or Black Mosque, which was once a part of Firozabad. The fort on the Jumna on the eastern side of the city is shut off from the outside world by its own red sandstone wall, over fifty feet high, more than half a mile by 1600 feet long. After passing through the great bastion of the Lahore Gate and a bazaar-hall where the royal bodyguard at one time performed their sentry duty, the visitor finds himself in the courtyards, chambers and gardens of the imperial residence. Only some of the buildings which Shah Jahan erected for himself and his court survived the decay that set in under the last of the Mogul emperors and the demolition carried out subsequently by British garrisons. It was Lord Curzon who launched a widespread campaign for the preservation of India's ancient monuments and exercised his viceregal authority to enforce the evacuation of the fort by the army and to set about the task of restoring it.

The last of Shah Jahan's masterpieces were The Great Mosque (Jama Masjid) opposite the Red Fort in Delhi and the Pearl Mosque in the Palace of Agra. The mosque in Delhi ranks as the largest in the Islamic world but here again it is not the external dimensions that excite our admiration and wonder but the superb proportions and the exquisite taste. Built on a vast substructure, which is surrounded by a wall with huge red sandstone gateways, the great marble courtyard, a haven of peace in the noisy city, is dominated by the three shimmering onion-domes over the prayer-hall and the two prayer-towers, which are visible for miles around. By contrast, the Palace Mosque at Agra does not strive for outward architectonic effect; it lies more or less secluded in the upper storey to the north of the great audience chamber. From the courtyard, in which form is completely lost in a blaze of light, one steps into the glimmering twilight of the prayer-hall, which is divided by three rows of pillars and three domes and is paved in marble, while the lighting produces an almost magical effect of delicate iridescence. A long inscription in black marble mosaic acclaims the successful completion of the building in the flowery language of the period, and one passage runs as follows:

> This is truly a sublime place of Paradise, shaped out of a single pearl. Never since there have been men upon this earth has a House of God been built so pure and entirely of marble to compare with this, since the creation of the universe no place of worship has appeared which could compete with this.

It was Shah Jahan's intention to build a tomb of black marble for himself on the left bank of the Jumna near Agra, which would combine with the Taj Mahal on the opposite bank to produce an effect of unusual grandeur, but, when he fell gravely ill in 1658, his son Aurangzeb, who had already disposed of his older brothers, seized power and had the deposed emperor removed from Delhi to his palace in Agra, where he was cared for by his daughter Jahanara till he died. He was buried by the side of his wife in the Taj Mahal.

Aurangzeb added another masterpiece to the palace buildings in Delhi, a palace chapel, the enchanting little marble Moti Masjid (pearl mosque), but the golden age of Mogul architecture was over. The emperor was engaged in a continuous struggle to defend and expand his vast dominions. A fanatical Muslim, he vented his hate on the unbelievers and gained melancholy fame by destroying a considerable number of Hindu temples. He built a mosque in Benares at the highest point on the bank of the Ganges, in order to proclaim the triumph of Islam even in this great place of pilgrimage.

Aurangzeb, a tired, trembling old man, haunted by fear of the last judgment, had barely breathed his last in 1707 when the struggle for the succession broke out and the empire, which had been so laboriously held together, began to crumble. In 1739 the emperor of Persia, Nadir Shah, arrived in Delhi, ostensibly as guest of the impotent Grand Mogul but in fact as a conqueror. When the inhabitants greeted him with stones, he let his soldiery loose on the city; when he left, he took with him the famous jewel-studded Peacock Throne, from which the rulers of Delhi had presided over royal audiences and dispensed justice. In 1803 the city was occupied by the British and from then on the emperor was fated to be no more than a figurehead. In 1857, when an army mutiny broke out with unexpected fury, Bahadur Shah, whom the British had left unmolested in his palace and who derived considerably more pleasure from poetry and beautiful women than from the crude art of war, allowed the mutineers to name him their leader; but the mutiny was suppressed as quickly as it had broken out; the last of the Grand Moguls, who had taken refuge in the tomb of his forefather Humayun, surrendered and spent his last days in exile in Rangoon.

Roughly half-way between Delhi and Patna, Asoka's capital, lies Lucknow, a key point in Sher Shah's empire, where the provincial governors declared their independence from the Mogul Empire when it collapsed in the eighteenth century and where they founded the kingdom of Oudh. The Nawabs, as the Muslim rulers were called, were, however, very soon dependent upon the goodwill of the British. It was the last of the Muslim provincial states and in Lucknow, for the last time, one of those conglomerations of gateways, palaces and mosques was built, which were designed for the lasting glory of a ruling dynasty—products of a late period, which are modelled on earlier masterpieces and built quickly and cheaply but which are nevertheless impressive if only for their spaciousness. In the year 1856 the British deposed the last of the kings, who had been ineffective as a ruler, and shortly afterwards the British garrison in Lucknow was hard put to it to ward off the ferocious attacks of the mutineers. The city, together with Allahabad, subsequently became the capital of the 'United Provinces' and is today the administrative capital of Uttar Pradesh.

Allahabad received its name in 1584 as one of the provincial capitals of the Mogul Empire but, in spite of its Islamic name, has remained since time immemorial a particularly holy place to the Hindus; for here is the confluence of the two great rivers, the Jumna and the Ganges, which flow through the most densely-populated plains of northern India. In January and February every year the pilgrims pour in, and every twelve years an immense throng of bathers celebrate Kumbh Mela. For the rest of the year the bathing-places of Tribeni are deserted, but lower down the Ganges at Benares (now Banaras or Varanasi) the flow of pilgrims never ceases. In India Benares is believed to be the oldest city in the world, its position on the Ganges between two tributaries, the Assi in the south and the Barana in the north, having

been chosen by Siva himself; both great epics mention it but there is no historical record of its remote past and any ancient monuments that may have survived were destroyed during successive Muslim incursions, the first of which was in 1033. But the Hindu who comes to Benares to be purified by the holy water and blessed by the grace of Siva is not concerned with the antiquity of earthly monuments in stone or script; the palaces and temples of the princes, which crowd the river bank, may fall into decay or become defaced by advertisements, they may reveal a mixture of styles and defy all aesthetic reason, he does not care, and the visitor, after an absence of thirty years, finds them as changed as the self-perpetuating vegetation. New flights of steps and niches continue to be built for those who want to pray apart from the multitude and the only thing that still counts is the throng of the faithful, who at sunrise hurry through the narrow alleys past the vendors of flowers and rose-garlands and the beggars to the ghats, where they perform their ritual exercises in the Ganges.

In Benares Siva is worshipped in the light-lingam as Visvesvara, the Lord of the Universe. He delivers the dying from the cycle of rebirth, and even the pilgrim who is still far from having attained the necessary degree of enlightenment can receive his full grace at this holiest of places. So Benares is also the place to which the infirm, the sick and the dying aspire. From the ghat below the Nepal temple, where the bodies of the dead are burnt, the smoke rises incessantly. Within twenty-four hours of the soul leaving the body, the corpse is brought on an open bier to the funeral pile, where it is sprinkled with holy water, while the sacred cows eat the garlands of flowers, then the next-of-kin lights the fire and the ashes are carried away by the river—and another pile is already belching smoke, a third funeral procession already approaching.

Only a few miles north of Siva's city with its endless sea of faces the traveller finds himself in the peaceful seclusion of Buddha's world, the world of the wandering monk who came here to set the Wheel of the Law in motion. A gigantic stupa has survived the ravages of time, archaeologists discovered the foundation-walls of the monasteries visited by Fah-hsien and Hiuen-tsang, and amongst other treasures which have been unearthed, the museum contains the magnificent capital from the pillar erected by Asoka in the Deer Park of Sarnath.

8 Fatehpur Sikri. Diwan-i-Khas, Akbar's private audience-chamber, also misleadingly known as Ibadat Khana or House of Devotion. In the foreground the pool in front of the 'House of Dreams'

9 Old Delhi, Mausoleum of Ghyas-ud-din-Tughlak (1320–25). Red sandstone with marble inlays and white marble dome

0 Old Delhi. Hauz-i-Khas, Mausoleum of Firoz Shah Tughlak (1351–89), restored by Sikandar Lodi in the early 16th century

1 Akbar's mausoleum at Sikandra near Agra. View from the gateway of the monument, which, according to an inscription, was completed in 1612 in the seventh year of the reign of Akbar's successor, Jahangir. The tomb was robbed in 1691

2 Old Delhi. The mausoleum built for Humayun, who died in 1556, by the architect Mirza Ghyas on behalf of Humayun's widow, Hamida Begum; completed in 1572. Red sandstone with white marble

3 Agra. Courtyard of the octagonal tower-pavilion Saman Burj in the imperial palace which was extended by Shah Jahan. Top left, the private audience-chamber Diwan-i-Khan. White marble inlaid with precious coloured stones

4 Agra. Hathi Pol, i.e. Gate of Elephants, the inner gate of the western main gateway (Delhi Gate), and main entrance to the fort with the imperial palace, built during Akbar's reign

5 Agra. The Hall of Prayer of the Pearl Mosque (Moti Masjid) in the fort, 150 ft wide and 55 ft deep; built in 1648–55 by Shah Jahan; white marble

6 Agra. Taj Mahal. In the middle of the main chamber under the shallow inner cupola stands the sarcophagus, surrounded by a marble screen and bearing the inscription: 'The splendid tomb of Arjmand Banu Begam, called Mumtaz-i-Mahal (the Jewel of the Palace), died AH 1040 (AD 1629). To the left of it is the sarcophagus of Shah Jahan, who died in 1666. In a vault underneath are the graves themselves in the same order

7 Agra. The Taj Mahal viewed from the gateway, as the architect intended the visitor to catch his first glimpse of the tomb, surrounded by its gardens and flanked by four minarets

8 Yakshi with birdcage; from a stone railing round a

stupa on Bhutesvar hill near Mathura (Muttra). Red sandstone; Kushana period, c. 2nd century BC. Indian Museum, Calcutta

189 Brindaban. The 'Red Temple' of 1590, dedicated to the Gobind Deo, i.e. the Divine Cowherd (Krishna)

190 Gobardhan. Bathing-steps in the Manasi-Ganga temple pool

191 Women at the well—a picture one sees constantly in the Indian countryside—between Agra and Delhi

192 On the old military road between Agra and Delhi

193 Old Delhi, Lal Kot. The Tower of Prayer and Victory, Kutb-Minar, 235 ft high, was started by the first 'Slave King', Kutb-ud-din; Iltutmish (Altamsh) continued the construction in red sandstone as far as the balcony on the third storey. After lightning had damaged the tower in 1369, Firoz Tughlak Shah covered the two top storeys with white marble

194 Old Delhi. Tughlakabad. The walls of the fortress planned by Ghyas-ud-din Tughlak

195 Old Delhi, Purana Qila, i.e. Fortified City, founded by Sher Shah to replace Din Panah, which had been founded before by Humayun. On the south side the great fortress wall is broken by a gate in red sandstone inlaid with marble

196 Old Delhi, Lal Kot. In the courtyard of the mosque Quwwat-ul-Islam, i.e. Might of Islam, which was started by Kutb-ud-din and continued by Iltutmish. Before the 50 ft high central arch stands the Iron Column of pure, rust-free iron, 23 ft high from its base. According to a Sanskrit inscription it dates back to the Gupta period and according to another inscription was brought here (presumably from Bihar) in 1052 by Anangapala and erected in his temple, to be taken over later by the Mosque

197 Old Delhi. Tomb of Sikandar Lodi (1489–1517), presumably built by his successor, Ibrahim Lodi; octagonal, typical of the domed tombs in the Pathan (Afghan) style with the double dome, high outside and more shallow inside

198 Old Delhi. The Mosque of Khirki, built in 1380 by Khan-i-Jajan Jumna Shah, son of Firoz Tughlak Shah's all-powerful minister, Khan-i-Jahan Tilagini. Monolithic columns carry the vaults round from symmetrically designed courtyards

199 Delhi, Shahjahanabad. In the palace buildings of the

Red Fort. In the middle of the rear wall in the public audience-chamber (Diwan-i-Am) is the niche where the Peacock Throne, stolen by Nadir Shah, once stood and where the ruler sat during his daily audiences, so that he could listen to what each of his subjects had to say

200 Delhi. Outside the gates of Shahjahanabad, in the heart of modern New Delhi, Jai Singh II, the scholarly maharaja of Jaipur, built one of his observatories (cf. plate 275), the focal point of which is the 55 ft high structure for observing the sun

201 Delhi. Entrance to the Sikh Temple Sisganj Gurdwara viewed from the main street Chandni Chauk. The temple was built on the spot where Aurangzeb executed the ninth guru, Tegh Bahadur, in 1675

202 Delhi. Entrance to the south gate of the Great Mosque (Jama Masjid)

203 Agra, Taj Mahal. Verses from the Koran carved round the entrance to the tomb

204 Delhi. The Great Mosque built in red sandstone and white marble by Shah Jahan 1644–48. View from the east gate across the courtyard, with the well of purification in the centre and in the background the Hall of Prayer crowned by three domes and flanked by two minarets 190 ft high

205 Fatehpur Sikri. Buland Darwaza, the south gate of the Great Mosque (Jama Masjid), added to the existing mosque as a Gate of Victory by Akbar after the conquest of Gujarat in 1573

206 Fatehpur Sikri. The house of Raja Birbal, most important of Akbar's Hindu collaborators, completed in 1572. As it adjoined the quarter reserved for the women, the house was possibly not occupied by the raja himself but by his daughter or one of the emperor's wives

207 Fatehpur Sikri. Interior of the Diwan-i-Khas (cf. plate 178) with the great central column, from whose broad console-capital four bridges lead to the corners of the gallery in the upper storey

208 Agra. Tomb of the Itihad-ud-dawla and one of his wives, built in 1622–28 by his daughter, the Empress Nur Jahan. The Persian Mirza Ghyas Beg, as Emperor Jahangir's treasurer, was called Itimad-ud-dawla

209 Agra. Imperial Palace in the Fort: one of the man ornamental panels at the entrance to Jahangi Mahal, a part of the palace dating back to Akba

210 Agra. Imperial Palace in the Fort: view from the roo of the palace on to the Anguri Bag and over th pavilions of the women's quarters; marble wit gilded roofs. In the background a bend of th Jumna and the Taj Mahal

211 Agra. Imperial Palace in the Fort: Diwan-i-An Shah Jahan's public audience-hall with stuccoe sandstone pillars

212 Lucknow. The Mosque of the Great Imambar built by Asaf-ud-Dawla (1775–97), who moved th Nawab of Oudh's capital from Fyzabad to Luckno

213 Lucknow. Entrance-hall to the Great Imamba built in 1794

214 Allahabad. Pilgrims congregate under the walls the Fort for the great Magh Mela pilgrimage, i order to bathe at the sacred place where the Jumn and Ganges meet

215 Benares (Banaras, Varanasi). Steps (ghats) on th Ganges waterfront leading up to the palaces an temples, which were founded at various times b various princes and repeatedly replaced by nev buildings

216 Benares. Pari Jalsain Ghat, the cremation-ground o the banks of the Ganges

217 Benares. A sadhu (Hindu ascetic) with Siva' crescent and trident

218 Benares. Beggars crowd round the main entrance t the sacred bathing-places

219 Benares. A sadhu with the Siva-symbol on his fore head and a garland of roses meditating in one of th niches provided in the waterfront wall, his fac turned towards the rising sun

220 Benares. A typical bathing-place

221 Benares. On the crowded steps a pilgrim become engrossed in reading the holy scripture

222 Benares. Bathing and praying on the Ganges

223 Sarnath near Benares. View across part of a excavated monastery of the Great Stupa or Dhamel Tower with remains of the outer coat of brickwor added during renovation in the Gupta period; th base is approximately 140 ft high, the lower part o stone, the upper part of brick

189 BRINDABAN

OBARDHAN

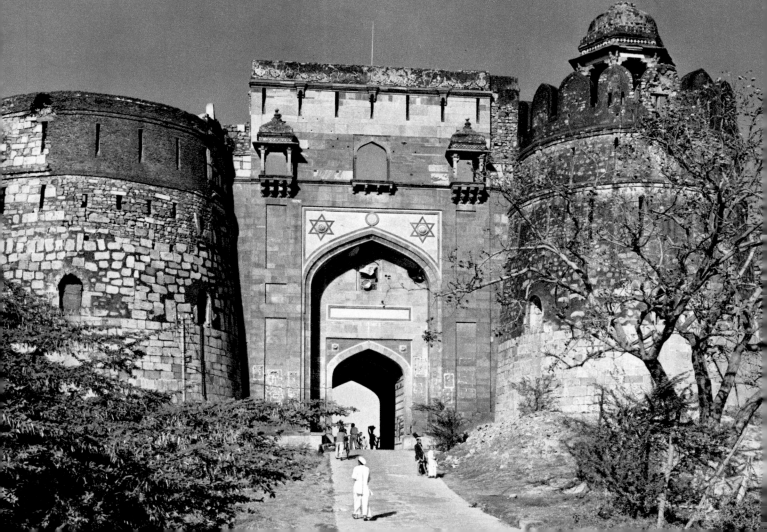

200 DELHI,
JANTAR MA

201 DELHI
GURDWARA
202 DELHI,
JAMI MASJ

203 AGRA, TAJ MAHAL

204 DELHI, JAMI MASJID

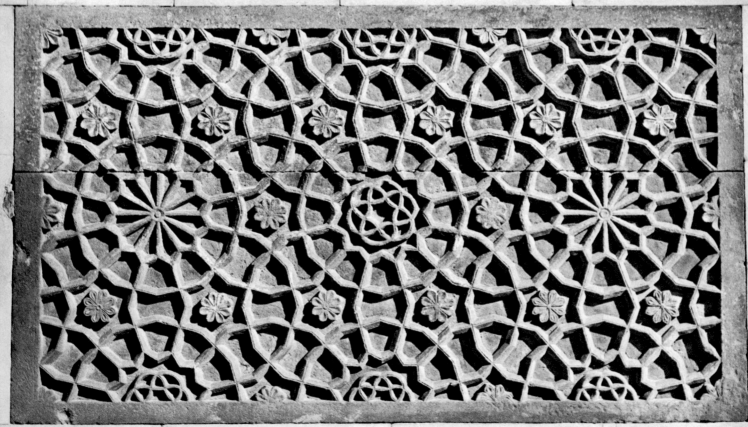

ALLAHABAD

BANARAS

216–222 BANARAS

217

218

219

220

221

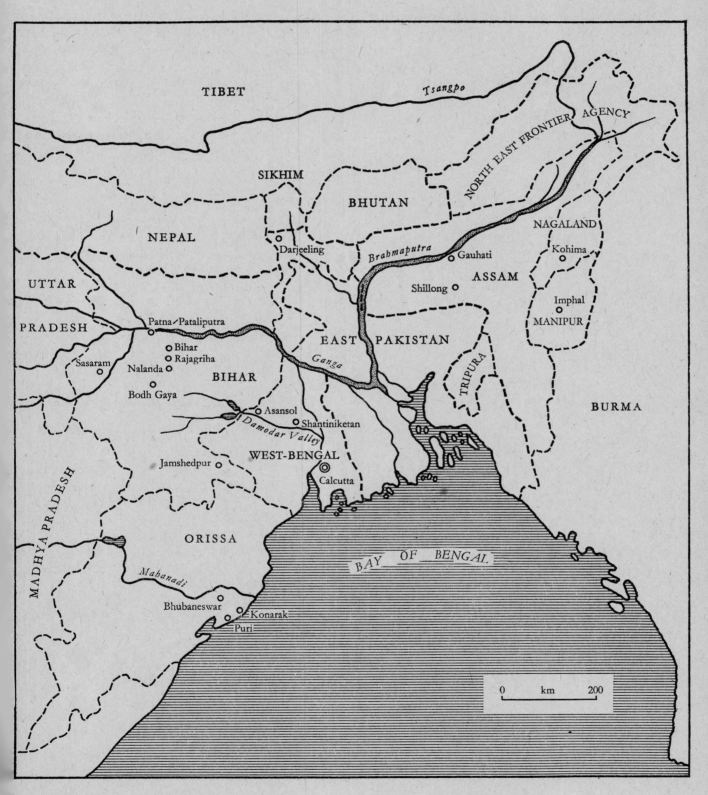

BIHAR
WEST BENGAL
ASSAM
ORISSA

TIBET

Tsangpo

NORTH EAST FRONTIER AGENCY

SIKHIM

BHUTAN

NEPAL

Darjeeling

Brahmaputra

Gauhati

NAGALAND

Kohima

ASSAM

Shillong

UTTAR

PRADESH

Patna – Pataliputra

Bihar

Rajagriha

Nalanda

Sasaram

BIHAR

Bodh Gaya

Imphal

MANIPUR

Ganga

EAST PAKISTAN

TRIPURA

BURMA

Asansol

Damodar Valley

Shantiniketan

WEST-BENGAL

MADHYA PRADESH

Jamshedpur

Calcutta

ORISSA

Mahanadi

BAY OF BENGAL

Bhubaneswar

Konarak

Puri

0   km   200

BIHAR WAS FORMERLY the kingdom of Magadha, which, in Buddha's lifetime, was ruled by King Bimbisara and where the great Emperor Asoka had his capital. In their accounts of their travels Fah-hsien and Hiuen-tsang give detailed descriptions of it and even today the traveller is made aware that he is at the birthplace of a world religion, where the Indian who was to help shape the future of human civilization experienced his first manifestation.

If one approaches the scene of Buddha's enlightenment, Bodh Gaya, from the holy city of Benares, one is confronted about half-way by the other power which also gives this part of India its dual personality. Just before reaching the Son, the broad stream that flows down to join the Ganges, the traveller arrives at Sasaram, where he finds himself standing before a building of unparalleled majesty: the tomb of Sher Shah. We have already encountered the great Afghan in his role as builder of Purana Qila, one of the cities of Old Delhi. It was here in Bihar that he began his rise to power. His proper name was Farid and he acquired the name Sher after killing a 'sher' or tiger during a hunt. His superior, the governor of Bihar, had declared himself independent of the kingdom of Delhi after the defeat and death of Ibrahim Lodi at Panipat and had assumed the title of sultan; he entrusted the scholarly Sher Khan, who was the king's representative at Sasaram, with the education of his son. Sher Khan proved more than a match for those who were intriguing against him, spent some time at Babur's court at Agra until he aroused the latter's suspicions, then, on the death of his patron, the sultan of Bihar, acted as regent for the young sultan, who was under age. Finally, by either out-manoeuvring his foes or beating them in the field, he took over the empire which Babur had established. He built his tomb in his native place as a monument to Afghan rule in India, which challenged that of the Moguls not merely on the battlefield but also in the art of statesmanship and even in architecture: surrounded by water, the domed tomb rises from the centre of a broad stone terrace—a style which the Lodi kings had already adopted in Delhi but which reaches its peak of perfection here, a remarkable achievement as was everything else that Sher Shah turned his hand to.

No figure, however, has ever so dominated India's vast landscape as the man who is commemorated in the sacred shrine with its temple tower at Bodh Gaya. India is, of course, no longer a Buddhist country, but Buddha still remains the son of the great Hindu family, he has spread far and wide beyond the seas the fame of India's wisdom, his image has become the symbol of the human struggle to achieve perfection by self-abnegation, and the Indian nation reveres him as the greatest of its sons.

His birthplace Kapilavastu lies in the Terai, a wooded strip of country at the foot of the Himalayas, which today on the Nepalese side of the Indian border. To the east of where the town once stood is the garden of Lumbini, where Maya (which means 'miraculous power'), holding on to a branch of the sala tree, gave birth to her son. Here a pillar was found, split down the middle—Hiuen-tsang tells us—bearing the following inscription from the emperor Asoka: 'Here Buddha Sakyamuni was born.' The legend has it that Buddha's father was a king, there seems no doubt that he came of a distinguished family. Maya died shortly after he was born and her sister Mahapajapati, another of Suddhodhana's wives, proved a devoted adoptive mother to the boy. The prince was brought up in an atmosphere of royal luxury. As was customary for someone of his position, he was given three houses, one for winter, one for summer and one for the rainy season; beautiful dancing-girls and musicians formed part of his court. He married a beautiful young girl and she bore him a son, Rahula, who subsequently became one of his disciples. But Siddhartha had already had the four encounters on four separate excursions which set him on the road in search of truth; in the frailty of old age, in sickness and in death he was made aware of human suffering, but in the spectacle of the wandering ascetic in his yellow cloak, head shaven, he saw a symbol of man's freedom. One night, at the age of twenty-nine, he left his sleeping wife and child. His faithful equerry Chandaka saddled his horse Kantaka and accompanied him as far as the gates of the town, where Gautama set off to walk barefoot with his begging-bowl the length and breadth of the land.

The search lasted seven years. He sat at the feet of the spiritual teachers, who were filled with secret knowledge, then he tried a life of extreme austerity in the solitude of the forest. Five other hermits joined him, filled with admiration for his asceticism, but they abandoned him in disillusionment when he became convinced that

225 PATALIPUTRA

226 NALANDA

austerities were serving no purpose and resumed normal eating and drinking, with the result that his body recovered its former beauty. Near Uruvilva, where the modern town of Gaya stands, he sat down under the Bo tree and abandoned himself to the profound meditation which was to mark the turning-point of his life. Mara, the great tempter, approached him in several forms, offering him all the pleasures of the flesh and even mastery of the world, then finally issuing fearful threats, but the Bodhisattva (the seeker after 'bodhi' or knowledge) repulsed him calmly. When Mara charged him mockingly that he had no evidence to show for his alms-giving, Gautama touched the ground with one hand and called the earth to witness and the earth replied with a great tremor. At last he was left entirely to himself. In the first night-watch he achieved awareness of his previous existences, in the second night-watch he acquired the knowledge of all living things, in the third night-watch he understood the chain of cause and effect which is the source of all evil, and at daybreak he attained complete enlightenment. He is alleged to have said of this period:

As I became aware of these things and as I saw these things, my soul was delivered from the corruption of becoming (in the cycle of rebirths), delivered from the corruption of false belief, delivered from the corruption of not knowing. In the delivered awoke the knowledge of deliverance: rebirth is destroyed, the sacred cycle fulfilled, the duty done; I shall not return to this world.

Two travelling merchants were the first to meet the Buddha and to recognize his holiness. He wandered on towards Benares till he reached the Deer Park at Sarnath, where he met the five ascetics again who had previously abandoned him. It was to them that he preached his first sermon and set the Wheel of the Law in motion.

Sarnath marked the beginning of a long period of renewed wandering with the beggar's bowl, a period in which countless conversions were made and the Order was founded. Princes and other notable personalities in public life were particularly attracted by the new doctrine, but the Brahmans, who were jealous of their priestly privileges, were slow to admit the generous teaching that people of all classes might hope for salvation. The Master was especially attached to the country round the city of

Rajagriha, where King Bimbisara of Magadha was one of his most faithful followers.

The India through which Buddha and his disciples wandered consisted of innumerable medium-sized, small or minute 'kingdoms', principalities and republican communities, over which even the great empires which emerged later exercised little real authority and then only at specific strategic points. Right up to the present time the one thing that has bound the countless village communities together into one single family of 'Indians', transcending all barriers of race and language, is the unceasing flow of pilgrims, which no political frontier has been able to stem. The fame of certain sacred shrines has proved stronger than even the most profound religious differences.

Buddha was eighty years old when his wandering finally ended. In a grove of trees at Kusinagara, east of the modern town of Gorakhpur, he lay down to die and entered into Nirvana. The highest honours were paid to the dead man, before his body, in accordance with Hindu custom, was surrendered to the flames. Eight tribes and princes divided the sacred ashes amongst themselves and at eight different points in India the first stupas were erected over the holy relics.

Shortly after Buddha's death his chief disciples are said to have held their first Council at Rajagriha, in order to give some doctrinal form to the Master's message. Here already the first differences appeared which were to develop more and more into separate schools and cults, a schism which neither the Council of Vaisali a hundred years later—presumably a historical fact—nor the determined zeal of the convert Asoka could heal. It is said that the emperor was at first antagonistic to the Buddha's teaching and even destroyed the shrine of Bodh Gaya and gave orders for the revered Bo tree to be cut down—but it may well be that someone else was guilty and that these actions were ascribed to him merely in order to make his entry into the Order more dramatic.

In the centuries before and after the birth of Christ Buddhism spread throughout northern India as far as Afghanistan and Ceylon. But Brahmanism, as early Hinduism was called, had by no means disappeared; on the contrary it too had taken on a new lease of life.

The Brahmans also worked out their own interpretation

of Buddhism, making Buddha the ninth and last of the great incarnations of Vishnu; according to this doctrine, Buddha should appear in the present fourth age of the world to encourage evil men by his false teaching to violate the precepts of religion and above all, of course, to violate the caste-laws, thereby ensuring their own destruction.

Mahayana Buddhism with its wealth of imagery clearly offered strong competition to the colourful world of the new Hinduism. The reports of Chinese pilgrims are full of legends, which had been built up in one of the holy places or in the crowded monasteries around the visit of some Buddha or around some relic. And the *Jatakas*, the stories relating to Gautama's earlier lives, also provided ample scope for the imaginative story-teller and for unascetic imagery.

At Nalanda, not far from Rajagriha, scene of the first Council, Kumaragupta founded a monastery in AD 427 which grew to become a complex of large monasteries and the main teaching centre of northern India. Fah-hsien mentions only one village with a pagoda in honour of Sariputta, one of Buddha's earliest disciples; but when Hiuen-tsang visited Nalanda, there were some ten thousand monks living there, and the Chinese pilgrim spent five years at this widely-known centre of learning, in order to enrich his knowledge at the feet of India's wisest men. Moreover, Nalanda was still flourishing when monasteries elsewhere were being abandoned and when the stone-masons at Ellora were no longer Buddhists but were hollowing caves and temples out of the rock in honour of Vishnu and Siva.

In 1193, when the Muslim conquerors reached Bihar and massacred the 'idolatrous unbelievers', the Buddhists were still in the majority on the lower Ganges. According to an eleventh century inscription, the great temple of Bodh Gaya had been restored by the Burmese—an indication that the native population had lost all interest. There are records to show that Buddhist monks were here until 1331, but even before that the temple itself had passed into the hands of the Brahmans; since the sixteenth century it has been the property of a Siva monastery and to this day it fulfils the dual function of a Hindu shrine and a place of pilgrimage for Buddhists of all denominations. Akbar's chroniclers do not even call the place

Bodh Gaya but Brahma Gaya. Buddhism in India had become just another sect like any other and almost slipped into oblivion, when a new age dawned with the arrival of the English.

Of the Buddhists outside India, the Burmese followers of Hinayana Buddhism in particular have never lost their attachment to the birthplace of their religion. In the years 1306–09, according to an inscription, they restored the temple of Bodh Gaya a second time, and again in the nineteenth century they were the first to undertake repair work on the shrine. On this occasion the central tower, which dominates the rest, was given a new facing—an oft-repeated process.

The restorers from Burma, who took only a secondary interest in art and architecture, were followed by the archaeologists. Under English patronage expert excavations and repairs were carried out at Bodh Gaya. Lord Curzon, the powerful viceroy whose outstanding work for the protection and maintenance of Indian art treasures cannot be denied even by his most violent critics, discovered in the residence of the Hindu Mahant twenty-three pillars from the stone railing which had been built around 184–172 BC. Following this discovery other fragments were assembled in their original position round the temple. The reliefs, which are swarming with figures, all depict scenes representing adoration of the Buddha, with Buddha himself, as was customary at this period, only appearing symbolically as the Bo tree or as a canopy.

After the turn of the century more and more visitors arrived from the Buddhist countries, especially adherents of Hinayana or southern Buddhism from Burma, Siam and Ceylon. Amongst the most zealous of the pilgrims are the representatives of Lamaism from Tibet, whose large new rest-house has become a regular meeting-place for Tibetans driven from their homeland. Mahayana Buddhism is represented by the occasional courtly delegation from Japan. The Indian Republic for its part has done everything in its power to maintain the sites of Bodh Gaya, Sarnath, and Nalanda with all the care that national shrines as such deserve and Bodh Gaya, for example, has recently been provided with gardens, rest-houses, an attractive tourist kiosk and a museum.

Fah-hsien wrote of Rajagriha, where King Bimbisara of Magadha placed a grove at Buddha's disposal for meditation and teaching and where, after the Master's death, the first Council is reputed to have taken place: 'Here indeed was the old city of King Bimbisara, which measured some five to six Li from east to west and eight Li from north to south. Today it lies abandoned, without a single inhabitant.' On the other hand this fifth-century Chinese pilgrim found the mineral baths of Rajgir fully operative:

On the south side of the mountain two warm springs emerge; the water is very hot. In the old days Tabhagata (Buddha) caused this water to spring forth and bathed in it. Since then it has flowed with the same purity and the same force. From near and far people throng hither to bathe and a number are cured of chronic ailments.

To this day one can still see crowds of visitors, who have come to refresh themselves at the warm springs in the Hindu temple. And farther up the mountain one can still visit, as Fah-hsien did, the old walls and the rock-caves, where the disciples of the Master who had entered Nirvana used to meet.

At nearby Nalanda the only building above ground is a gigantic stupa which towers over the place that for centuries was a meeting-point for scholars. The foundation walls of the great monastery-complex with its courtyards and cells have been uncovered by the archaeologists and they give some idea of the importance of this school of learning as Hiuen-tsang describes it in his enthusiastic report of the seventh century:

The priest-monks, of whom there are several thousand, are men of the highest ability and virtue. Hundreds of them have acquired widespread fame by reason of their spiritual gifts. The rules of this monastery are strict. The day is never long enough for question and answer on the most profound problems. The discussions continue from morning until evening; old and young alike take part. Learned men come hither from all manner of places in order to excel in these discussions and to allay their own doubts ...

We must draw even more on our imagination if we are to conjure up a picture of Chandragupta Maurya's capital, Pataliputra, the foundations of which were excavated outside the gates of Patna, the present capital of Bihar: fragments of pillars from a great hall, a few palisades and other finds are all that remain of the splendid capital which the Greek ambassador Megasthenes described (his original report has only survived in the form of quotations by Strabo and others). The palace with its gilded pillars stood in a magnificent park in which peacocks and pheasants roamed, meals were served in huge golden dishes, and the king would appear, surrounded by a highly colourful retinue, in a golden litter or enthroned on an elephant.

BENGAL was the most unruly province in British India. The Muslims had already started invading the ancient Brahman Kingdom while the first Slave Kings were ruling Delhi and ever since then the country has been exposed, as no other part of India has been, to the split between Hindus and Muslims. Even the British rule failed to heal it. Lord Curzon tried partition in 1905 but this merely brought popular emotions to the boil. After the British withdrew, the radical solution was adopted of separating East Bengal, which went to Pakistan, from West Bengal with its restless capital Calcutta.

Bengal has none of those awe-inspiring monuments in which India is so rich, but as a collection of Indian works of art the Indian Museum in Calcutta is still unique of its kind. The Bengalis are a restless people; their enemies regard them as unreliable, cunning and cruel, but, however that may be, in recent years they have produced some of India's outstanding politicians, scientists and artists, such as C. R. Das, a founder of the Swaraj Party which for some time dominated the Congress movement, Ramakrishna and Vivekananda, two of the most prominent spiritual leaders of the new Hinduism, Ram Mohan Roy, founder of the Brahma Samaj religious community which goes back to the Upanishads and condemns idolatry and the caste-system, and the remarkable Tagore family (known to the would-be connoisseur as Thakur!).

The Tagores had at one time been expelled from the Brahman community, because they had established friendly relations with Muslims. The Semindar (Lord of the Manor) Raja Dwarkanath Tagore joined Ram Mohan Roy's movement; his son Devendranath became its spiritual leader; he was known throughout India as 'Maharshi' or the Great Sage and he established himself at Shantiniketan near Bolpur, where he spent all his time in meditation and which his son Rabindranath later turned into a meeting-place for like-thinking men from all countries, a sort of international university. The circle which grew up around this great poet produced a renaissance of all the arts, from painting and poetry to music and drama. Rabindranath's nephew Abanindranath, who lived in Tagore's Calcutta palace, was a no less fascinating personality and a considerable painter. The journey to Shantiniketan also enables one to see something of Bengal's villages with their curved thatched roofs, which are derived from an ancient style of architecture copied in the early rathas of Mahabalipuram.

West Bengal today stretches as far north as the frontiers of Sikkim on the threshold of Tibet. In Darjeeling, seven thousand feet up, where British governors retired when Calcutta became too hot for them, the traveller who has come all the way from the southern tip of India finds himself in a new world: the clouds which frequently wreath the mountains bring abundant rainfall and with it a climate in which the leaves of the delicately-scented Darjeeling tea flourish. Stocky little Mongols with round, smiling faces throng the market place: Lepchas and Bhutias, people from Sikkim, Nepal and Tibet, lamas clothed in felt and carrying their prayer-mills, and, mingling with them, the Bengalis from the plain, shuffling along, draped in white. But with luck the clouds will break at sunrise and for brief moments, like some phenomenon from another world, the white peak of Kanchinjunga will appear, as if riding in the sky.

Few tourists find their way into Assam, into the valley of the Brahmaputra in the extreme north-west, for not only is it surrounded by impenetrable jungles but it is almost completely cut off from the rest of India by East Pakistan. The frequent rainstorms occasionally lead to floods, and earthquakes are not uncommon. Since the thirteenth century the Muslim rulers of Delhi had tried in vain to occupy the country, and every newspaper reader knows that the present Indian government has to employ every means it can in these areas to make its authority felt. The capital, Gauhati, was almost completely destroyed in the earthquake of 1897 but some of the temples in the surrounding country which survived are fine examples of the local architecture, and the great flight of steps leading down to the Brahmaputra, which opens out here as it

approaches the sea, is visited by pilgrims from far and near who come to this place to bathe.

The old kingdom of Orissa on the Bay of Bengal, capital of the Kalingas who were brutally conquered by Asoka, was one of the 'five Indias' which Harsha subdued to form into a single kingdom in the seventh century. After the sultans of Delhi had turned neighbouring Bengal into a province of Delhi, the Hindu kings managed to survive right up to the time of Akbar; they intervened on many occasions in the wars for the control of the Deccan and even allied themselves from time to time with their religious opponents.

The capital, Bhubaneswar, had been an important religious centre since pre-Christian times. Buddhists, Hindus and Jains hollowed out their caves in the rocky hillsides round the capital, sixty-three of them in all and the most important group of its kind in north-west India. Then during the renaissance of Hinduism in the middle ages thousands of large and small shrines sprang up along the shores of the holy sea, and between the eighth and thirteenth centuries appeared the incomparable collection of temples which made the art of Orissa world famous. One must not expect the Hindu architects to solve their construction problems as they were solved by the use of the arch and the vault in constructing tombs and mosques; in their sastras they followed quite different rules and designed their shrines and towers like sculptures in which the groins and mouldings repeat the general motif over and over again in minute ornamental detail, not unlike a classical composition in music; the carvings are nothing like so lavish as at Khajuraho. Over the 'deul', the innermost room with the sacred image, rises the beehive-shaped tower called the 'rekha'; stretching in front of it as a rule is the Bhadra building with the entrance-hall or 'jag-mohan' and a roof that mounts in terraces in the form of a pyramid. The most imposing of the temples constructed to this design is the Lingaraja, which was started in the seventh century and completed in the eleventh century. Here Siva is worshipped under the form of the Swayanbhulinga, the self-procreating lingam, as Tribhubaneswar, Lord of the Three Worlds. Rivalling the Lingaraja in holiness is the Jagannatha Temple at Puri, a neighbouring place of pilgrimage. Since time immemorial this temple has been associated

228

229

230

231

with miracles. The god dwelling here, who on ceremonial occasions is honoured in special processions but who for the remainder of the year is still worshipped by pilgrims from all parts of the country, is an incarnation of Krishna–Vishnu as 'Lord of the Universe', and although strangers are forbidden to pass through even the outer gate, they can at least see the group of sacred images with the strangely primitive image of Jagannatha, his somewhat bigger brother and little sister in the many popular reproductions.

Temple-architecture in Orissa reached its peak in the reign of King Narasimha Deva (1238–64) with the construction of the 'Black Pagoda' of Konarak in a solitary position on the shore. Twelve wheels larger than man-size complete the illusion of an immense stone chariot carrying the sun-god Surya. The tower over the deul has long since disappeared or may never have been completed—Fergusson, the first man to explore India's architecture, saw a section of it still standing in 1837 but thirty years later it had disappeared, so today it is the entrance-hall with its pyramid roof that is the dominating feature. Overwhelmed as one is by the monumental proportions of the entire structure, one is no less amazed on looking closer by the apparently inexhaustible—and highly erotic—fantasy and the creative inspiration of the skilled craftsmen, who covered these walls with reliefs of gods and amorous couples, dancers and musicians, herds of elephants, hunting and battle scenes.

NOTES TO THE PLATES

224 Sasaram. The tomb of Sher Shah, who died in 1545. Set in a square pool, it has a dome 150 ft high

225 Pataliputra near modern Patna. Remains of one of the halls in the palace built by Chandragupta and extended by Asoka

226 Nalanda. The excavated foundation-walls of a monastery with its individual cells

227 Bodh Gaya (Buddha Gaya). The eastern approach to the Great Temple, which has undergone several alterations, on the scene of Buddha's Enlightenment

228-231 Bodh Gaya. Sculptures on the stone railing (Sunga period) round the shrine. Plate 228 shows the Bodhi tree representing the Buddha as the Enlightened One

232 Bhubaneswar. Bathing-place on the sacred pool Vidusagar, i.e. 'Drops of the Ocean', which is surrounded by shrines of every size

233 Bodh Gaya. Votive stupa of Mahayana Buddhism near the great temple

234 Bodh Gaya. The stone railing (cf. plates 228–231) at the south-west corner of the temple; above it the branches of the Bodhi tree (ficus religiosa), under which (or under its predecessor) Buddha sat when he attained Enlightenment

235 Bodh Gaya. Tibetan pilgrims before the Vajrasan or Diamond Throne under the Bodhi tree on the west side of the temple

236 Sarnath. A lama and another Tibetan pilgrim walking round the Great Stupa

237 Nalanda. The Great Stupa

238 Nalanda. Padmapani, also called Avalokitesvara, one of the Bodhisattvas of Mahayana Buddhism, who preceded the historical Buddha. Sandstone; c. 800. Nalanda Museum

239 Rajagriha, the modern Rajgir, capital of King Bimbisara of Magadha. View from the hillside, where the first Council is said to have been held after Buddha's death. Below is the Hindu temple with hot springs, well known since ancient times

240 The hot springs of Rajgir (Rajagriha)

241 The fertile, densely-populated Ganges plain around Patna is irrigated from ancient wells

242 A village in West Bengal with typical Bengali roofs

243 Peasant sitting outside his mud-hut covered with palm-leaves, in a village in Bihar

244 Assam. Hindu temple at Gauhati

245 Gauhati, capital of Assam. Bathing-steps and temp on the Brahmaputra

246 Darjeeling. Young Lepcha woman in the market

247 Darjeeling. View at sunrise of the Himalayas wi the 28,146 ft high Kanchenjunga

248 The Dakshineshvara Temple (19th century) ne Calcutta, where Ramakrishna, one of the Hinc revivalists, lived and taught

249 Shantiniketan in West Bengal. The library buildir of the international university founded by Rabin ranath Tagore (1861–1941) in 1910 in his father house, which he subsequently extended

250 Shantiniketan. A female member of the Tago circle with the vina, India's classical instrument

251 Konarak (Kanarak). The temple of the sun-gc Surya, called the Black Pagoda (as distinct from tI White Pagoda, the Jagannath Temple of Puri built during the reign of King Narasimhadev (1238–64)

252 The sun-god Surya from the temple of Konara Museum of India, New Delhi

253 Konarak. One of the two gigantic lions which a seen bounding over elephants and apparent drawing the sun-god's chariot

254 Konarak. One of the twelve wheels of the temple

255 Puri. The Jagannath (Juqarnath) Temple, S Mandir

256 Bhubaneswar. The great Lingaraja Temple, which its present form dates back to c. AD 1000 with tl 180 ft tower (sikhara) over the shrine of tl Tribhunavesvar (Lord of the Three Worlds); front, the gatehouse and assembly hall (Jagmohan in the temple precincts around the main building a a number of smaller shrines

257 Bhubaneswar. The Muktesvara Temple

258 Bhubaneswar. A sadhu with rose-garland seated c the tiger-skin (Siva's) in front of his cell

259 One of the caves in Udayagiri (Sunrise) Hill ne: Bhubaneswar

260 Bhubaneswar. A naga on one of the temples

261 Bhubaneswar. House of a Brahman, newly-painte for the New Year

262 Village in Orissa

263 Young pilgrim at Puri

234

233–235 BODH G
236 SARNATH

237–238 NALANDA

238

239-240 RAJAGRIHA
240

242 WEST-BENGAL

249

249–250 SHANTINIKETAN

251 KONARAK

252 KONARAK, SURYA

255 PURI

259

259–260 BHUBANESWAR

261

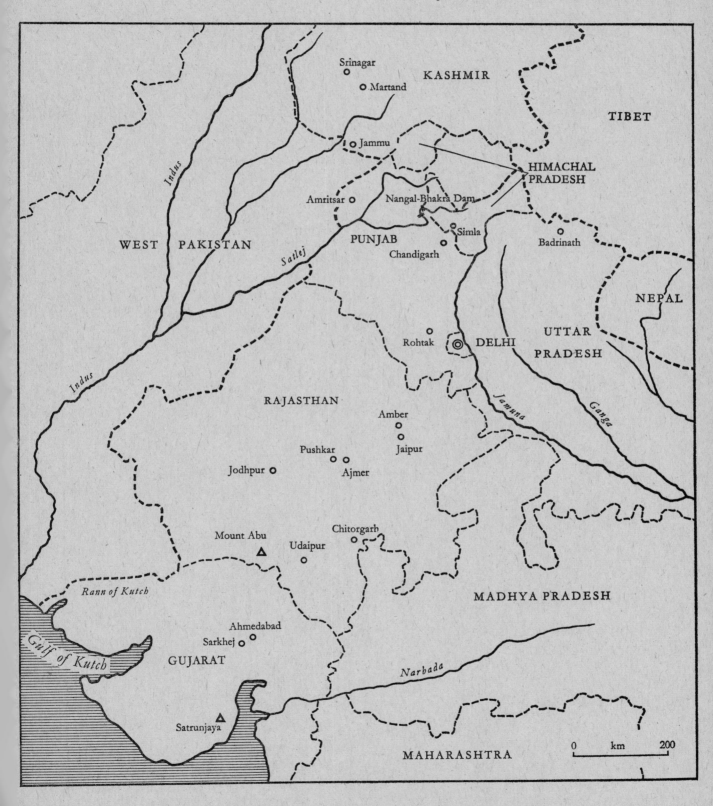

RAJASTHAN
GUJARAT
PUNJAB
JAMMU AND KASHMIR

Srinagar
Martand
KASHMIR
TIBET
Jammu
HIMACHAL
PRADESH
WEST   PAKISTAN
Amritsar
Nangal-Bhakra Dam
Simla
Indus
Satlej
PUNJAB
Chandigarh
Badrinath
NEPAL
UTTAR
PRADESH
Rohtak
DELHI
Indus
RAJASTHAN
Jamuna
Ganga
Amber
Pushkar
Jaipur
Jodhpur
Ajmer
Chitorgarh
Mount Abu
Udaipur
MADHYA PRADESH
Rann of Kutch
Ahmedabad
Sarkhej
GUJARAT
Narbada
Gulf of Kutch
Satrunjaya
MAHARASHTRA
0   km   200

RAJASTHAN (RAJPUTANA) IS the land of the rajas, of the princes, great and small, who ruled over a tall, warlike people. The maharajas for the most part retained their independence both in the Mogul Empire and under the British rule; they consorted with the emperor on an equal footing, their beautiful daughters represented the most distinguished matches in India, and their courts rivalled those of Agra and Delhi in brilliance. Only a few decades ago one could still meet the men in the public squares with their brightly-coloured turbans and martial beards, carrying the slightly curved Rajput sword with its beautiful hilt; but today they no longer parade their traditional pride quite so openly. The princely states have been absorbed by the republic and twentieth-century bureaucracy has also crept into Rajasthan, but it is still one of the most picturesque countries in the world, with countless large and small castles and palaces, with the brightest of flower-markets and saris, with camels pacing placidly through the streets and bazaars full of glittering necklaces and glowing fruit. There are also, of course, plenty of temples but they do not predominate as they do in other parts of India where Hinduism never lost its supremacy. Here man rises, self-assured, above the manifold wonders of creation, builds palaces and gardens to his own individual taste, paints Krishna and Radha on the walls of his house almost as if they were members of his family and tells stories of the heroic deeds of forefathers, who are not shrouded in legend. The rulers, at the same time, feel the need to match the splendid tombs of the Muslims with some monuments of their own, so the maharajas of Jaipur build the chhatris with their marble domes on the burning-places.

The heroic deeds of the Rajputs are particularly closely linked with the fortress of Chitor, seat of the rulers of Mewar from the eighth to the sixteenth centuries. The fortress fell three times and on each occasion the defenders made history. Three times they were overwhelmed by superior forces and the women committed 'jauhar' by casting themselves into the flames, while the men stormed out of the gates and died fighting; it happened in 1303 when Chitor was besieged by the sultan of Delhi, Ala-ud-din Khilji, again in 1535 when the sultan of Gujarat, Bahadur Shah, invaded the state, and finally in 1567 when Mewar was overrun by Akbar. The ruins of

palaces and temples in the precincts of the fortress indicate how important Chitor was as a princely residence. Near a Jain temple stands the 'Tower of Fame', which was buil in the twelfth century in honour of Adinath, the firs Tirthankara. And in the fifteenth century Rama Kumbha built the nine-storey 'Tower of Victory', lavishly decorated with Hindu sculptures, to commemorate hi victory over the sultan of Malwa (1440). When Chitor fel for the third time, the surviving member of the ol princely family moved his capital to Udaipur, the 'City o the Sunrise'. The 'maharana' traced his descent back t the legendary Indo-Aryan King Manu and his so Iksvaku, the king of Ayodhya, and as a descendant of th 'solar line' he carried the sun in his coat-of-arms; he wa by tradition accorded the highest rank among the Hind princes and, when the twenty-second maharana, Bhupa Singh, handed over the reins of government to the ne state of Rajasthan in 1948, he was the last of a line whic had survived all the invasions of India since the conque of Chitor by Bappa in 734.

Maharana Udai Singh founded the modern city Udaipur, which was named after him, in 1567 on Lak Pichola, which one of his forefathers, Maharana Lakha had created at the end of the fourteenth century, an between the sixteenth and the nineteenth centuries th enormous palace-complex was built, which is sti reflected in the waters of the lake today. There are als two small islands, on one of which Prince Khurra during the period of exile that followed his revolt again his father Jahangir, erected buildings and laid out garde which show the impeccable taste he later revealed Shah Jahan. The royal capital 'with its snow-whi palaces and pavilions, its flower-gardens, shady grove enchanting lakes and wooded islands', which even su sophisticated travellers as Pierre Loti and Lord Curzo regarded as unique, has even today lost nothing of i romantic charm, and any visitor to whom expense is object can even invite himself to stay at one of the islar palaces, which has been converted into an hotel.

Among the royal seats of the Rajputs the fortress Amber with the neighbouring city of Jaipur also has distinguished history. The maharaja is the head of t Kacchawaha clan of the Rajputs and traces his desce back to Kush, the eldest son of Rama. Prithvi Raj (150

) had resisted Babur's invasion but his successors made
peace with the Moguls, and with the marriage of Raja
Bhar Mal's daughter, Miriam-zamani, to the great Akbar
and the subsequent birth of the future emperor Jahangir,
the Hindu prince of Amber became one of the strongest
powers behind the throne of Delhi. Raja Man Singh I
(1589–1614) became commander-in-chief of the Mogul
army; he laid out the splendid palace on the rocky hilltop
of Amber. Jai Singh I (1627–67) held a similar position in
Delhi as general and statesman to that held by Prince
Eugene at the Imperial Court at Vienna. But the most
fascinating of the Kacchawahas was Jai Singh II (1669–
1743). When he came to the throne at the age of thirteen,
he paid his respects to the Grand Mogul in Delhi. The
distrustful Aurangzeb received the young Hindu very
ungraciously but was so won over by the quickness of his
repartee that he said to him: 'You surpass even your
predecessor Jai Singh I in intelligence and ability, you are
sawai (i.e. one-and-a-quarter-fold)!' From then on the
maharaja was known as Sawai Jai Singh. He had an
excellent command of the Persian court language of the
Moguls as well as of classical Sanskrit, was interested in
history and law, and also found time, in addition to his
duties in the Mogul Empire whose ruler was largely
dependent upon him following Aurangzeb's death, to
introduce reforms in his own state. He completed the
palace buildings at Amber, which were fitted out as
splendidly as any Mogul residence, and on the open plain
he laid the foundations of a new city, which was better
suited to the state's administrative, economic and com-
munications requirements than Amber, tucked away in its
narrow valley: this is Jaipur, which was named after him
and is not only the present government capital of
Rajasthan but also, apart from New Delhi and Chandigarh,
the most spacious and 'most modern' of India's cities; in
planning the city, the learned architect consulted both the
Silpa Shastras, in which the old Indian principles of
architecture are to be found, and Europeans who came to
his court and were able to inform him on town-planning
in the West. The wide, straight streets provide ample
room for camel-caravans and automobiles, and the
universal pale pink of the buildings, which has given rise
to the name 'Pink City', gives it a festive, gay appearance
which is enhanced by the riotous colour of the flower and
fruit-stalls at the central crossroads. But Jaipur's really

unique feature was the product of its builder's passion for
mathematics and astronomy. In four places—Jaipur,
Delhi, Ujjain and Benares—Sawai Jai Singh built
observatories, the largest in his own capital, which were so
constructed as to make possible the most precise observa-
tion of sun and stars that was conceivable before optical
instruments came into use.

Amongst Rajasthan's other cities Ajmer also deserves
special mention. Although the state of Ajmer, named
after Ajayameru, the 'impregnable hill', had enjoyed a
period of great prosperity in the Middle Ages only to lose
its independence to the Muslim invaders and come under
a series of different masters till it was finally surrendered
to the English in 1818, the city itself enjoyed great
prominence as one of the favourite residences of Akbar
and his two immediate successors, and to this day it is
famous as the burial-place of the most revered Muslim
saint in India. Khwaja Muin-ud-din Chishti, who was
born in Ghor in Afghanistan, home of the conqueror
Muhammad, had come to Ajmer in 1490; the spirit of
kindliness and compassion which this ascetic radiated was
so in keeping with the Hindu ideal of the saintly life, that
the fame of the pious Muslim spread far outside his own
religious community. Iltutmish, the powerful sultan of
Delhi, built a tomb for him which soon became a place of
pilgrimage and which Shah Jahan, builder of the Taj
Mahal, crowned with a marble dome. Akbar, who used
Ajmer as a military base from which to control Rajasthan
and Gujarat, made regular pilgrimages to the saint's
shrine between 1570 and 1582.
Outside the sacred precincts stands the second great sight
of Ajmer, the mosque of Adhai-din-ka-Ihonpra. When
Muhammad of Ghor conquered the city, he had a hall
which had been built by the Jains for a religious school
converted into a mosque and Iltutmish built a seven-
arched wall in front of it, which reminds one of the finest
monuments in Old Delhi and which has Kufic and
Tughra characters interwoven with abstract ornamentation. Shah Jahan's advanced sense of décor can also be
admired on the banks of Lake Anasagar, an artificial
lake which Raja Anaji was responsible for making around
the middle of the twelfth century: Jahangir had laid out
a garden there and his son added the marble quay with
five elegant pavilions.

Only seven miles from the Muslim place of pilgrimage lies the Lake of Puskara, which is particularly sacred to the Hindus; it is mentioned in both the great epics and Fah-hsien remarked upon the large number of pilgrims. It is the place where Brahma, the god of creation worshipped in ancient Brahmanism, assumed earthly form and where, when he let fall a lotus flower, water sprang up out of the ground. The temple erected in his honour is the only noteworthy Brahma shrine in India. The religious fanatic Aurangzeb wrought havoc among the shrines on the Lake of Puskara but he failed to destroy the sanctity of the place, and, although the new temple-builders lacked the artistic originality of their predecessors, they at least showed just as much zeal in honouring the resident divinity.

In the south-western tip of Rajasthan and on the Kathiawar peninsula, which belongs to Gujarat, we find two of those remote mountains on which, as we have seen at Sravanabelgola and Sonagir, the Jains so often built their shrines: the twelve hundred feet high Satrunjaya in what was once the small principality of Palitana ranks as the most sacred of the mountain-temples of the Jains, and Mount Abu with its Dilwara temples, four thousand feet up in a mountainous landscape, is the most magnificent specimen of its kind.

Abu had been since legendary times a centre of the Siva cult, until the tenth and eleventh centuries when the Jains left their imprint on the place. The two most important of the five Dilwara temples date, in one case, back to 1031 when it was founded by Vimal Shah, a man of simple origins who rose to high office under the Chalukya dynasty, and, in the other case, to 1230, when it was consecrated, after having been built, according to the inscriptions, by Tejapala, a minister of the king of Gujarat. Both are strikingly alike in that, while the exterior is remarkably plain, the interior teems with decorations in shimmering white marble; ceilings and pillars are covered with carvings and sculptures of divine beings and animals as delicate as woodwork, and statues of the Tirthankaras, studded with precious stones, stare blankly from the many niches.

The Jain temples of Satrunjaya go back to the eleventh century, but such was the destructive fury of the Muslim conquerors that little remains of the earlier buildings; it was not until the end of the fifteenth century, when a more tolerant atmosphere set in, that religious foundations underwent a revival and any visitor blessed with riches— and there were not a few of them among the Jains—was encouraged; as a result, particularly in the sixteenth century but also later on, temple after temple, large and small, was built, till finally 863 of them crowned the mountain-peaks. Here one walks barefoot over the naked, spotlessly clean tiles, stepping up from one courtyard to the other, through an oppressive stillness that is broken only by the beating of wings and the twittering of birds. The occasional white-clad priest or pilgrim has a cloth tied over his nose and mouth, for he is forbidden to destroy any form of life and even the tiniest insect must not be harmed.

It did not occur to Mahavira, any more than it did to his famous contemporary Buddha, that he should found a religious order, when he actively promoted the Parsvanatha sect, which presumably already existed, and became the 'Jina' or Spiritual Conqueror and the twenty-fourth and last 'Tirthankara' or Pathfinder with Adinath as the first and the presumably historical Parsvanatha as the last of his forerunners. Like Buddha, it did not occur to him that temples would be built in his honour or godheads worshipped. He preached deliverance from the cycle of rebirth, which was only attainable through monastic asceticism. Like Buddha he practised in the region of Bihar, yet presumably neither was aware of the other's activities. The followers of Mahavira also broke up into various sects. Their main centre was transferred to Gujarat, but the doctrine did not spread beyond the borders of India; it always remained much more closely linked with the great Hindu community than Buddhist doctrine with Buddhism.

The Jains are well known for their high ethical standards of conduct and their liberality. The vows which bind members of the Order are extremely strict: no creature, whether large or small, whether mobile or immobile, may be harmed; they must avoid and prevent the sin of lying wherever possible; they are not only forbidden to steal but must not tolerate it in others; they must abstain from any form of sexual activity, 'whether it concern heavenly, human or animal creatures', and all personal property is denied them.

odern Gujarat only dates back to 1960, when the state
Bombay was divided and the preponderantly Gujarati-
eaking population were given the administrative
itonomy which they had been demanding and which
emed justified by the distinguished history of the
ingdom of Gujarat. Before the capital Ahmedabad (also
lled Ahmadabad), one of the largest and most active
ties of India, became a modern industrial and com-
ercial centre, it bore the unmistakable stamp of the
iltans, whose capital it was until Akbar conquered
ujarat in 1572, and whose splendid buildings developed
a 'Indo-Saracen' style of their own. Ahmed Shah
411–41), the second sultan of the kingdom, after it had
aken off the rule of Delhi, founded the new capital on
e site of the ancient Hindu city Asaval. Ahmedabad,
amed after its founder, was hailed enthusiastically by
uropean travellers as an Indian Venice, a city 'as large as
ondon'.

he Gujaratis' part in the history of the new India has
en outstanding, if for no other reason than that both
ahatma Gandhi and Vallabhbhai Patel, Nehru's strong
ght-hand in building up the republic, came from this
istrict. Very near the capital, on the opposite bank of the
barmati, lies Satyagraha Ashram, where Gandhi, in the
ecisive stage of his career, lived with his closest
llowers, a hive of industry and propaganda and a place
f meditation, where I myself was privileged on one
ccasion to talk to this remarkable man and to see him
rn his spinning-wheel—the wheel of *his* teaching.

hile I was preparing this book, India's language
roblem made it necessary to divide up yet another of the
ates conceived by the architect of the new India.
lthough the old Punjab had already been split into a
akistani part—with the old capital Lahore—and an
idian part—with the new capital Chandigarh—the
unjab and Hindi-speaking districts have now also been
parated. The fault does not, of course, lie entirely with
e language problem. The Punjab is essentially Sikh
ountry; at Amritsar they have their Golden Temple;
iey are one of the most active communities in India, a
llar of strength to the Union, and their spirit of inde-
endence, which even enabled them on occasion to set up
n independent state, is the result of centuries of hard
ghting.

At the beginning of the sixteenth century the wandering
preacher Baba Nanak (1469–1538) founded the sect,
which today embraces several million followers and which
derived its name from the Sanskrit word Sisya or disciple.
Like Buddha, Mahavira and countless founders of
smaller sects before him, Nanak was a product of the
great family of Hinduism; in striving to free the teaching
of divine truth from all polytheistic associations, he also
adopted certain ideas from Islamic Sufism. He preached
humility, self-discipline, searching of the heart and
surrender to God; but he saw God as 'true, eternal,
indivisible, invisible, pure', not as Rama nor Allah and
belonging to no one people or no one religion, but the
God of the Universe and of all men. Nanak denounced the
idolatry and caste-system of the Hindus but continued to
believe in reincarnation.

Nanak is regarded as the first guru (teacher); he was
followed by altogether nine other gurus as leaders of the
main sects. The first four gurus, whose high office as a
rule was carried over from the father to the most eligible
of his sons, led lives of asceticism devoid of any worldly
ambition. They were loyal subjects of the Mogul
emperor. Under the fifth guru, Arjan (1581–1601), the
number of conversions showed a marked increase and
the Sikhs became a powerful organization, a state within
the state. The guru lived in Amritsar like a king, surrounded by a bodyguard, and here on the site of the
present Golden Temple he built the first house to
accommodate the sacred book, the *Adi Granth*, and
completed the two sacred pools. The Granth, which was
compiled by Arjan, contains the teachings and hymns of
Nanak and his immediate successors as well as religious
songs composed by several Hindu saints and the Muslim
Farid. Later on contributions by the ninth guru were
added and in 1734 a second collection of similar texts was
published, the Granth of the tenth guru. In the struggle
between Jahangir and his son Kushru for the throne,
Guru Arjan supported the latter and was tortured to death
in 1606 by the victorious Jahangir. His son and successor,
Har Govind (1606–45), became interested—and interested
his followers—in the art of war and built up his bodyguard into a small army. What had once been a relatively
harmless sect now became a people of warriors.

During the lifetime of the ninth guru, Tegh Bahadur,
Aurangzeb attempted to convert the non-Muslims by

force. When the Sikhs defended their temples against destruction, the guru was thrown into prison in Delhi and, as he stubbornly refused to embrace Islam, was tortured for five days and then beheaded (1675). The gulf between Muslim and Sikh was now unbridgeable.

In 1664 Tegh Bahadur had purchased from one of the small mountain-princes the strategically favourable site on which he built Anandpur Sahib, the 'holy city of joy'. His son, Govind Singh, the tenth and last guru, lived here for about twenty-five years. In this remote place he abandoned himself to meditation and gathered around him a group of fighting men, who were also religious fanatics and whose numbers steadily increased in spite of persecution. On 30 March 1699 the guru summoned the Sikhs from all parts of the country to Anandpur in order to organize them into a religious body called the 'Khalsa'. The first five of the elect, after having passed an incredible test of courage, were baptized with a handful of consecrated water and received the surname of Singh. They were bound to observe the five Ks; *Kes*, a ban on hair-cutting, *Kacch*, the wearing of narrow, knee-length trousers (much more practical for fighting than the normal Indian garb), *Kara*, the wearing of an iron armband, *Khanda*, the carrying of a small sword and *Kanga*, the wearing of a comb. They swore to help the poor and to fight oppressors, to believe in God and to renounce caste, dogma and superstition. The five Singhs then baptized the guru and on the same day twenty thousand men entered the Khalsa community.

In 1704 the guru had to give up his fortified retreat and the troops of the Mogul emperor destroyed the sacred buildings. The guru's four sons fell in the more or less continuous fighting, and in 1708, when Govind Singh himself was stabbed by an Afghan, he left his community this message: 'Wherever five Sikhs are gathered together, I shall be among you!'

The warlike spirit of the Sikhs, who belong for the most part to the sturdy Jak tribe, has remained alive to this day. Ranjit Singh (1780–1839) welded the loose republican confederation into a powerful kingdom. On the whole he got on well with the English, whose chief enemies, like his own, were the Afghans and the Gurkhas of Nepal. His successors, divided amongst themselves, failed to consolidate the Sikh state, which his military genius had created. In 1845 they were misled into attacking the English, whose forces under Sir Hugh Gough managed to hold their own at the battles of Ferozeshah, Aliwal and Mudki, then in the battle of Sabraon the Sikh army was finally defeated. The treaty signed at Lahore on 9 March 1846 recognized the Sikh Kingdom under Duleep Singh, who had finally emerged as maharaja from the bloody struggles for the throne, but, after an initial period of self-restraint, the English took a firmer hold of the reins in the Protectorate. In 1848 the murder of two British officers led to a renewal of the war and on 21 February 1849 Lord Gough gained a decisive victory at Gujarat. This marked the end of the Sikh rule; on 30 March 1849 the Punjab was annexed by the British. But they succeeded in making friends with the Sikhs again; these tough fighters became some of the finest troops in the British army and the British High Command even attached particular importance to the recruitment of devout Sikhs who had been consecrated by the sword or baptized. In helping to suppress the Mutiny of 1857, their old antagonism towards the Muslim rulers of Delhi came to the fore again and the prophecy ascribed to the ninth guru when he was taken prisoner by Aurangzeb was fulfilled: he should keep his eyes turned to the west, whence the Europeans would cross the sea to destroy his power.

In the eighteenth century the temple situated in the 'Nectar Pool' of Amritsar and the shrine at Anandpur were both destroyed but only to be rebuilt shortly after, and in 1802 Ranjit Singh placed the gilded copper roof over the shrine of Amritsar, in which the original of the Granth is kept.

The sons of Sikhs only become members of the community when they have been consecrated by the sword; should they not wish to submit to this solemn act of baptism, they revert to the great family of the Hindus. In the strong sense of loyalty which binds members of the faith together there is also an element of nationalism, and talk of freedom and self-determination has revived memories of the heroic period when they had their own state and has given birth to a political movement.

It is difficult for a foreigner to speak of Kashmir, if he feels a deep affection and friendship for both India and Pakistan. The mere fact that this book also covers Kashmir may offend the Pakistanis; to omit it would, however, have infuriated Indian patriots. The Hindu maharaja of Jammu and Kashmir with its preponderantly Muslim population had opted for India when 'partition' came, and, so far as the Indians are concerned, there is therefore no legal problem. The Pakistanis, for their part, are still waiting for the plebiscite which was suggested at one time. And the rest of the world is still hoping that the two opposing sister-nations may reach some friendly agreement. In the meantime, we cannot forego a visit to Kashmir and to the 'Happy Valley' of Srinagar.

Unlike the other Himalayan countries, Kashmir has always been easier of access to immigrants: in the third century BC Buddhist missionaries arrived here as emissaries from the Mauryan Empire. In the eighth century the oldest remaining temples were built, which show the influence of the Graeco-Indian style, and in the same epoch the king, whose power extended into the Punjab,

acknowledged the sovereignty of the emperor of China. The valleys of Kashmir lay right in the path of the nomadic invaders from central Asia, but the Hindu princes were able to hold their own until the early fourteenth century, when a Muslim seized power. In 1591 Akbar occupied the mountainous country and the Happy Valley was Jahangir's favourite summer resort. In 1739, when Nadir Shah of Persia plundered Delhi, he also annexed the territories from Sind to Kashmir; then Kashmir came under Afghan rule until 1819, when the Sikh leader Ranjit Singh conquered it. In 1846, after the defeat of the Sikhs by the British, the governor-general, Sir Henry Hardinge, made the Rajput prince of Jammu, Ghulab Singh, ruler of Kashmir, and it was his final successor who, in keeping with his Hindu faith, made such a fateful decision.

NOTES TO THE PLATES

264 Chitorgarh (Chitor). Jaya Stambha, the Tower of Victory, built in the years 1458–68 by King Kumbh of Mewar after his victory in 1440 over Mahmud Khilji of Malwa; 120 ft high, decorated with figures from Hindu mythology

265 Jaipur. Hawa Mahal, the Palace of the Winds, extended by Maharaja Mahdo Singh I (1751–68)

266, 267 Udaipur. The doorways of many houses are decorated with paintings on the white plaster, which are repainted on festive occasions; they keep alive the tradition of Rajput painting, which employed similar themes in the miniatures of the 17th and 18th centuries, a particular favourite being the blue-skinned Krishna with Radha

268, 269 Jaipur. Flower-market at a busy street-crossing

270 Ahmedabad (Ahmadabad). One of the two 'swaying minarets' of Sidi Bashir's mosque

271 An ox-cart on a country road in Rajasthan

272 Deeg (Dig). The Fort

273 Deeg. The palace buildings with pool built by Suraj Mal of Bharatpur, and the Gopal Bhawan pavilion of 1763

274 Chitorgarh. Kirtti Stambha, the Tower of Fame, the older of Chitor's two towers, from the 12th century, dedicated to Adinath, the first Tirthankara, and covered with Jain figures. Left, the Jain temple

275 Jaipur. View from the top of the Samrat Yantra, the gnomon for observing the sun, looking down on the other observatory buildings erected by Jai Singh II (1718–34) and on the hills surrounding the town, along the summit of which fortifications can be seen

276 Udaipur. A money-changer at the roadside

277, 278 Amber. Steps leading up to the Thakurji (Vishnu) Temple and one of the figures on the lavishly sculptured pavilion in front of the temple

279 Amber. View of the palace built by Man Singh I seen from the garden-pavilion on the pool below the castle hill

280, 281 Inside the Amber palace: the rooms over the fortified walls are richly decorated with paintings, inlaid glass and marble reliefs, the latest done in the reign of Jai Singh II, partly influenced by the Mogul emperors' palaces. In the top picture Ganesa

282 Gethur near Jaipur. Chhattri of Jai Singh II, who died in 1744—a memorial in white marble designed like a tomb and erected to commemorate the maharaja who was cremated here

283 Udaipur. The palace which Maharana Udai Singh started to build on Lake Pichola after the fall of Chitor in 1567 grew under his successors until it achieved its present vast proportions in the 19th century

273 DEEG

JAIPUR

JAIPUR

278

AMBER

279 AMBER

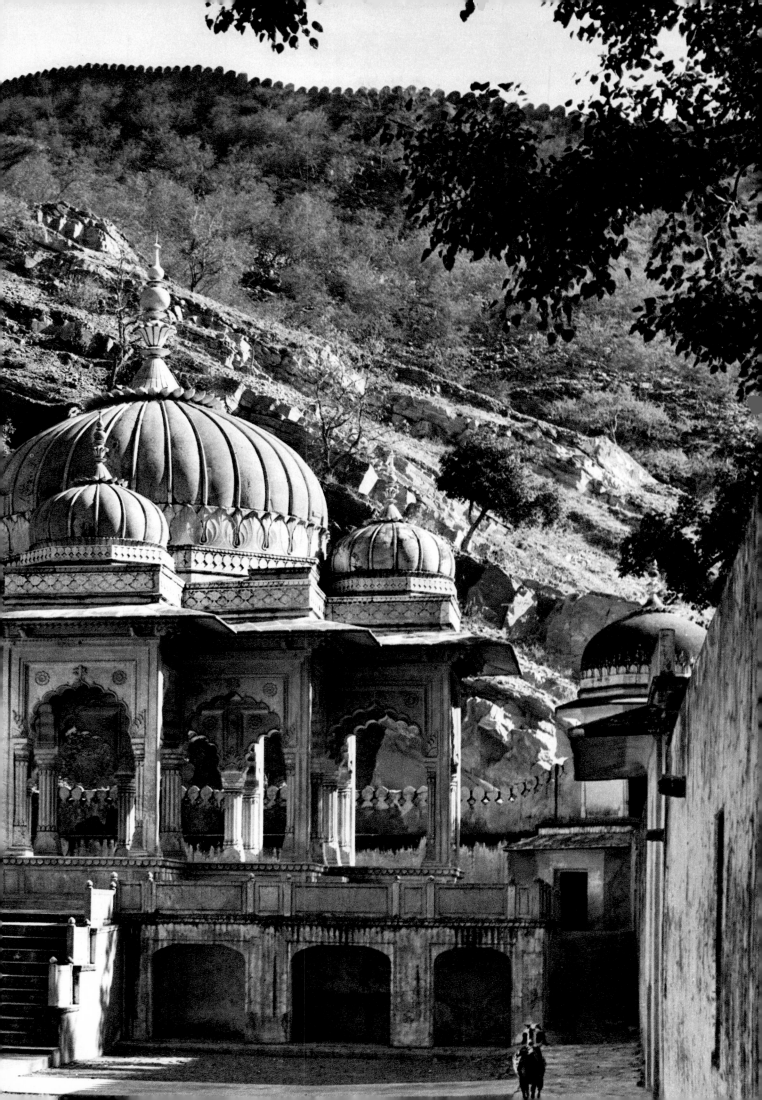

283-285 UDAIPUR

289–290 PUSHKAR

290

291 SATYAGRAHA ASHRAM

292 SARKHEJ

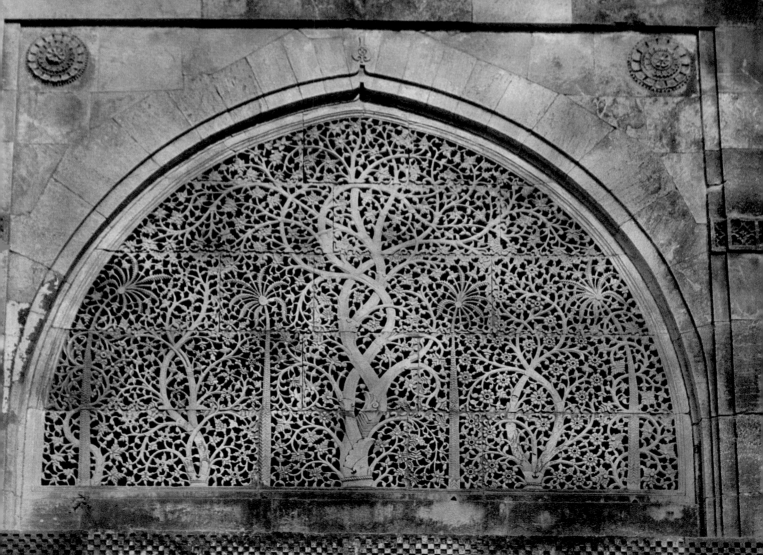

296-298 AHMEDABAD

297

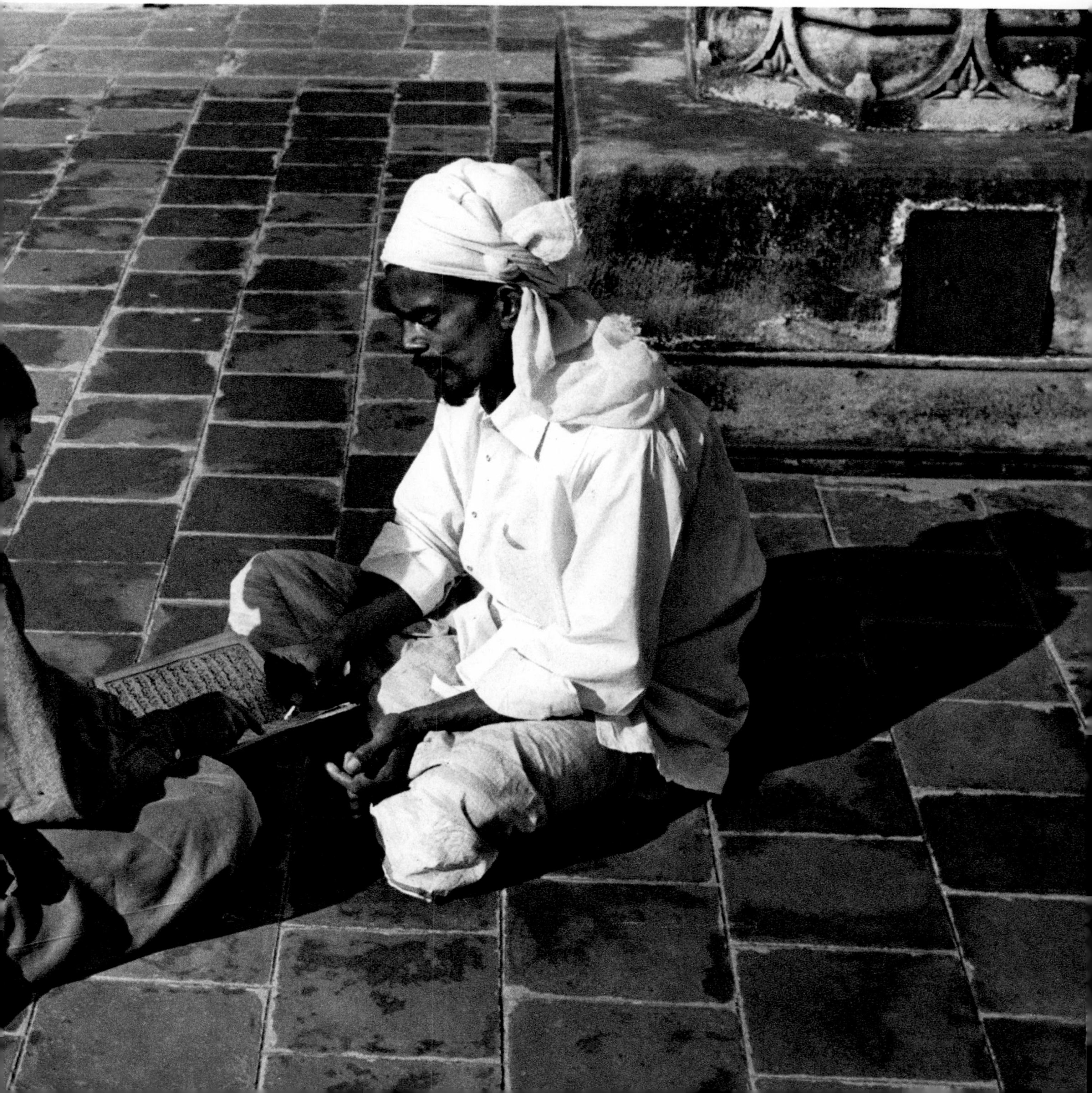

299 SATRUNJAYA

300 SIHOR, KATHIAVAR

301-303 MOUNT ABU

305 PUNJAB

306 GHARAUNDA

307 PUNJAB

310 ANANDPUR

311 AMRITSAR

312–313 AMRITSAR

313

314 JAMMU

315 MARTAND

316–317 SRINAGAR

317

318 BADRINATH

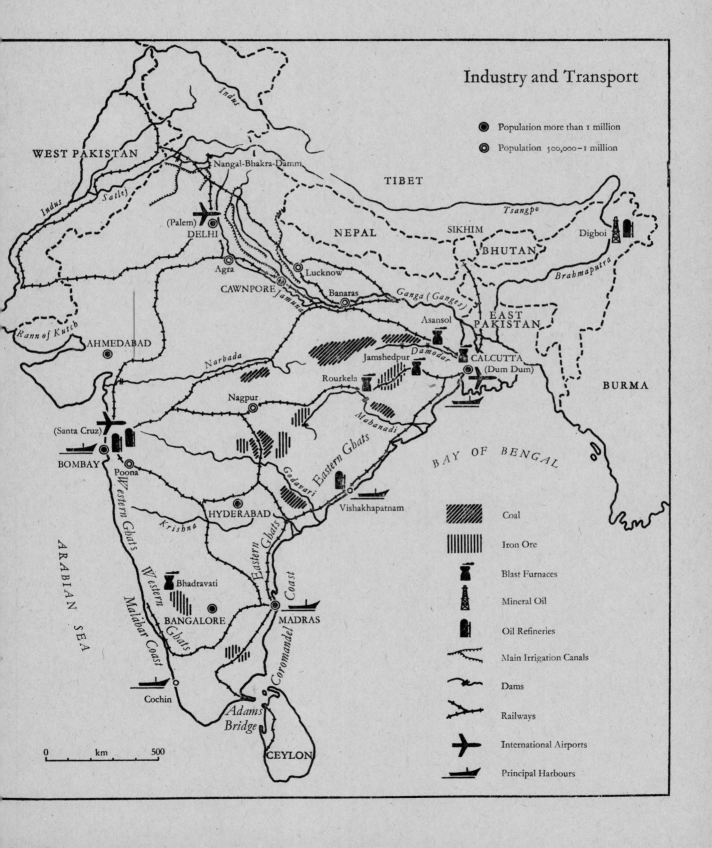

THE NEW INDIA

Industry and Transport

- ◉ Population more than 1 million
- ◎ Population 500,000–1 million

WEST PAKISTAN

Indus

Satlej

Nangal-Bhakra-Damm

TIBET

Tsangpo

(Palem)

DELHI

NEPAL

SIKHIM

BHUTAN

Digboi

Agra

Lucknow

Brahmaputra

CAWNPORE *Jamuna*

Banaras

Ganga (Ganges)

EAST
PAKISTAN

Rann of Kutch

Asansol

Damodar

CALCUTTA

AHMEDABAD

Narbada

Jamshedpur

(Dum Dum)

BURMA

Rourkela

Mahanadi

Nagpur

Eastern Ghats

(Santa Cruz)

Godavari

BAY OF BENGAL

BOMBAY

Poona

Vishakhapatnam

HYDERABAD

Krishna

Coal

Western Ghats

Eastern Ghats

Iron Ore

Malabar Coast

Bhadravati

Coromandel Coast

Blast Furnaces

BANGALORE

MADRAS

Mineral Oil

ARABIAN
SEA

Oil Refineries

Main Irrigation Canals

Dams

Cochin

Railways

*Adams
Bridge*

International Airports

0   km   500

CEYLON

Principal Harbours

ON OUR JOURNEY from south to north, from the Lingam Temple at Rameswaram to the Himalayas, on whose icy peaks Siva has sat wrapped in meditation for thousands of years while the Ganges streams from his hair, we have made our pilgrimage from temple to temple, to mosques and palaces which have outlived their past glories; here and there we have peeped into the cell of Indian life, the village with a pulse-beat that has barely quickened for centuries; we have followed in the footsteps of the Aryan invaders from shrine to shrine and picked up the traces of the Islamic conquerors from tomb to tomb; but one feature of India's natural landscape which we have not yet considered is the third invasion which is still in progress. For there is more to it than just the arrival and departure of the British pro-consuls. Much more important was the world-civilization which found its way in from the West and has continued to exert its influence ever since. With it came, to begin with, merchant-adventurers, new firearms and London Wren churches; then manufactured goods from Lancashire, new models of firearms, railways, an empire and ideas of nationalism, free trade and democracy. Then followed the gospels of self-determination, laicism and socialism.

In the Delta on the Bay of Bengal, where the waters of the Ganges and the Brahmaputra join, the first fort was built on the Hooghly river in 1696; in 1774 Warren Hastings, who had been governor of Bengal for two years, entered Fort William as the first governor-general of the East India Company, and around the fort, the harbour and shrine of Kali grew Kali-Kata or Calcutta, to become the largest city in India. In the eighteenth and nineteenth centuries the government and commercial buildings, hotels, banks and museums were built round the wide, green space of the Maidan. White pillared façades from London created a second Graeco-Indian style. In 1724 the Armenian community built the first Christian church and in 1783–87 the Anglican Cathedral of St John was built. The city attracted men of all classes, Hindus and Muslims, who came to seek work, and Chinese also made their way to this gateway to the Far East, a new urban life developed, in which the rigorous traditions of the village community lost their power; factories sprang up to refine the jute from East Bengal, an industrial proletariat emerged and side by side with it an intellectual class which evaded none of the problems that were troubling the outer world. In 1781 Warren Hastings founded the Sanskrit College and in 1784 Sir William Jones founded the Asiatic Society, which in turn produced the Asiatic Society of Bengal and a tradition of Indo-European research which was something new in India. 1786 saw the foundation of the Botanical Gardens, 1824 the Hindu College which since 1855 has been called Presidency College, 1853 the Medical College Hospital, 1857 the University; in 1875 the Indian Museum became the main repository of India's great cultural past, and finally the Victoria Memorial, a grandiose marble structure completed in 1921, was a mixture of Renaissance and 'Saracen' styles which demanded, somewhat too blatantly, comparison with the wonders of Mogul architecture. European scholars visited and described the abandoned sites of ancient Indian culture, deciphered the inscriptions, organized an archaeological service, and through them India discovered her past. But Calcutta also became the centre and power-house of a new revolution of a kind that India had never experienced before. Today even an Englishman would hesitate to describe the achievement of British Imperialism in such glowing terms as the Indian historian Kavalam Madhava Panikkar has described it:

During the time of the Company a great administrative machinery had been gradually built up, the foundations of which were laid by Cornwallis. The period that followed the Mutiny witnessed the growth and development of this administrative machine which has no parallel in the history of the world . . . The great all-India services, the I.C.S., the Indian Police, the Indian Audit and Account Service, the great provincial services (especially Revenue and Judicial services) created an administrative machinery which shouldered the burden of governing three hundred million people, which no government had actually faced before. The organization of such a vast machinery, which felt itself competent to deal not only with the work of government but with famine, plague, floods, etc., was possible only because of the historic tradition of

* 'A Survey of Indian History' by K. M. Panikkar (London 1947).

304

bureaucratic government in India, inherited from the time at least of the Mauryas. Only a small fractional percentage of the services was European. The rest was at all times recruited from the same class on which the previous empires of India had also depended: the Brahmins, the Kayasthas and the Khatris in the North, and the Brahmins and certain other literate castes in the South. Without the loyal assistance of this class . . . the organization of the great bureaucracy would not have been possible. With an administrative machinery so organized the Government was able to take up the work of government on a scale which no government outside Russia in recent times had undertaken. Railways and telegraph lines knit the country together. Great irrigation schemes were undertaken, notably in the Punjab and in the United Provinces. Peace reigned over the land, and law was administered as between man and man under a system of jurisprudence which was enlightened and comprehensive. The land revenue system was overhauled and, though an uneconomic system of landlordism prevailed in many parts, the settlement and assessment of lands and the Government demands from the ryots (peasants) were clearly defined. In fact for a hundred years India had a peaceful administration.

The Anglo-Indian administrators were not, of course, prepared to carry their reforming zeal to the point of risking a direct clash with the time-honoured way of life of the village population or to the point where their masters in London seemed likely to derive no profit. So while 'suttee', the burning alive of widows, was forbidden as a particularly repellent practice, the problems of the Untouchables, exploitation by moneylenders and other customs were treated with much greater circumspection. And the Anglo-Indians also had no interest in investing in industries, whose products might have offered serious competition to a mother country, which was dependent on its exports. On the other hand, when someone as enterprising as J. N. Tata (1839–1904) emerged in Bombay from the highly cosmopolitan community of the Parsees (followers of Zoroaster who came originally from Persia), then it was possible, long before the British left, for a native industrial concern to be built up on a massive scale.

Madras had a British garrison even before Calcutta. In 1639 Francis Day, with the approval of the raja of Chandragiri, last representative of the Kingdom of Vijayanagar which had once been so powerful, established an East India Company settlement, and next to Fort St George the town of Madrassapuram was built and its 'Corporation' was given a royal charter by the king of England in 1687. Farther south the French founded Pondicherry in 1674 on a site bought from the king of Bijapur. In 1693 they were driven out by the Dutch but they returned four years later and under T. F. Dupleix (1741–54) Pondicherry became prosperous enough to rival Madras. Had the ambitious French governor had his way, it would have become the capital of a great French India, but in the wars during the latter part of the eighteenth century the English gained the upper hand and although France had her Indian possessions restored to her in 1817, she never succeeded in turning her main port and administrative centre into more than an idyllic provincial capital, whereas Madras was developing into a modern commercial metropolis and the cultural centre of the Tamil-speaking Indians. In 1952 the Franco-Indian colonial empire was liquidated and the Indian national flag was hoisted over the Prefecture of Pondicherry.

Parallel with the development of Madras, Bombay had acquired a virtual monopoly of the traditional trade along the west coast, since it was ceded to the British by the Portuguese in 1665, and with the opening of the Suez Canal it had become more and more of a western-type metropolis. At the Apollo Bunder, next to the historic, multi-storey Taj Mahal Hotel, the 'Gateway of India' was built, where departing viceroys were in the habit of handing over to their successors as they landed.

The three great ports were not only gateways to world trade, they were also focal points of contact with foreign countries, bustling with intellectual activity, and it was here that the country's new intellectual élite emerged. Inland cities such as Bangalore in the south with its pleasant mountain climate, Hyderabad, the key-city of the Deccan, Nagpur, Cawnpore (now called Kanpur), Patna and Ahmedabad also played their part in the development of the new urban culture, and the day-to-day activity of a thriving city had the effect of quietly eroding many a deep-rooted social custom.

When Lord Curzon had to celebrate the accession to the throne of Edward VII in 1901 he summoned the princes of India to a great Durbar at Delhi and ten years later George V came in person to have the crown of India placed on his head in the ancient imperial capital. And the heart of the new India was to lie not where the seafarers and trading companies had built their forts but in the place which stands enthroned in the north of the country, with the Himalayas and the upper courses of the sacred rivers behind it and the vast triangle of the Deccan before it. It was here, next to this city of the Slave Kings, the Tughlaks, Firoz Shahs, Sher Shahs and Shah Jahans, that a new Delhi was to emerge as a lasting memorial to the India which had been united under the British Raj.

But while the viceroy was looking round for a suitable site amongst the ruins of Old Delhi and an army of workers was preparing to carry out the magnificent plans of the architect Sir Edward Lutyens for a city with wide avenues and handsome government buildings, demands for an early end to the British Raj were already being heard.

In 1927 the Indian Lower House, which was subject to the viceregal veto, met for the first time in the circular parliament building with its three chambers, and year by year more government buildings, notably the two enormous wings of the 'Secretariat', were built. Finally the domed viceregal palace was completed at the top of the main avenue that runs up Raisina Hill and on 15 February 1931 the official opening ceremony took place. No less a person than Le Corbusier, to whom the style of these buildings must have seemed outmoded, confessed thirty years later that the achievement of the British architects commanded respect and that it had been carried out 'avec un soin extrême, avec un grand talent, avec un véritable succès'.

When was the 'new' India born? On 15 August 1947, when the Indian Independence Act of the Parliament of Westminster became law and the two new dominions of India and Pakistan were created? Or on 26 January 1950, when the Legislative Assembly of New Delhi passed the new republican constitution? These two events were the result of a long historical process that went before they gave rise, and will go on giving rise, to other historic events. The withdrawal of the British was a mile-stone on a road which is still being built. Even the most orthodox Hindu politician would not dream of reverting to the sort of situation that prevailed before the incursion of European civilization, even though he may have his doubts about the degree of adaptation necessary. Most nationalists would have liked a more rapid process of Europeanization; they wanted more colleges and universities, faster means of communication, more factories and banks of their own, which would enable them to become masters in their own house. The final disappearance of a foreign tutelage which for decades had been systematically reduced gave a tremendous boost to the ambitions and plans of India's leaders, and anyone who visited the country twenty years after 'partition' was bound to notice significant changes everywhere.

As in any other country, the changing times are reflected above all in the cities: the commercial buildings of Calcutta, amongst which cows still pick their leisurely way, have become taller, Bombay is in the grip of a veritable building-fever, and in this cosmopolitan world of concrete palaces the occasional roof or pavilion in the Mogul style is a touching reminder that individuality has not been entirely swamped. The turrets and Gothic furbelows of the Victorian buildings have come to assume quite a historic appearance, with a character that is just as Indian as it is British. In Bangalore, capital of the new State of Mysore, it was decided that the parliament building should be on traditional lines and a gigantic four-storey palace was constructed in the most pompous Maharaja style with the lions from the Sarnath column on the central tower as the Republic's emblem.

Over the dome of the palace built in New Delhi for the viceroy flies the president's standard and here one can witness the parade of the mounted-guardsmen as they take over sentry duty: trotting along to the music of a military band, in red uniforms and carrying pennoned lances, with the occasional brisk command ringing out, they might almost be riding at Buckingham Palace. Civil servants in their fluttering white garb stream out of the government buildings: in Connaught Place—now officially called Indra Chauk—which is ringed about by a wide circle of pillared arcades, posters and a general bazaar atmosphere have taken some of the stiffness out of this London formality. The Anglican Cathedral of the Redemption with its austere splendour has a somewha forlorn look. On the other hand, the main Hindu temple in the new city, which owes its existence to the generosity of the Indian industrialist Jugal Kishore Birla and is therefore commonly known as 'Birla Mandir', is a hive of activity. It is dedicated to Laksmi Narayan, the goddess of beauty and temporal riches, and reminds one of the temples in Orissa; it was opened in 1939 by Mahatma Gandhi together with the Buddhist temple next door, whose tower was modelled on the shrine of Bodh Gaya. The temple of Laksmi is open to Hindus of all denominations and castes; these sacred halls are imbued with the spirit of the modern Hindu reformers, whose religion is essentially humanitarian.

New Delhi, as the centre of national planning, has also acquired something of the Anglo-Saxon imperial austerity which was a feature of the old bureaucracy; there is an air of cleanliness and correctness which comes from secular enlightenment, and the respect which was once accorded to the dignified viceregal peers has been replaced by a respect for authority, which is based on veneration of one outstanding, wise and perhaps even holy personality.

The enthusiasm of India's new planners freed of their foreign guardians is reflected even more strikingly and more clearly in Chandigarh, their very own creation, than in the rapidly expanding capital with its constant stream of visitors from all parts of the world, business men, technicians, politicians, Congress members and tourists.

When, with the decline of Lahore, the question arose of giving the Indian Punjab a new capital, a site was chosen at the foot of the Shivalik Mountains, not far from the former viceregal residence at Simla. The new city was to be a monument to a forward-looking concept of the state, untrammeled by an association with the past, and Le Corbusier, the most famous exponent of modern architecture, was brought from Paris to work out the general design. Backed by the great prime minister in Delhi and actively supported by the head of administration, P. N. Thapar, and the city engineer, P. L. Varma, Le Corbusier got down to work with his cousin Pierre Jeanneret and a team of Indian and British collaborators: the 'anatomy' of the city as he saw it consisted of the head in the form of government buildings, the body in the form of residential quarters, in the centre of which lies the municipal administration, and the feet were represented by an industrial area separated from the city proper by a green belt. Like the princely town-planners of ancient India, the twentieth-century planners also included an artificial lake as an integral part of the landscape. In the government buildings massive concrete blocks are arranged in a way that reveals the hand of the master himself; the Palace of Justice was the first to be completed, followed by the imposing 'Secretariat', and the whole is crowned by the Parliament buildings and the Governor's Palace.

Outside the large conurbations one can also find growing evidence of the interest in building: dams and power-stations, such as the huge Bhakra Dam not far from Chandigarh, canals and factories are proudly displayed as tokens of economic development, and, as one travels over the expanding network of roads, one is liable to come upon a college or agricultural institute in the most unlikely places, in a deserted part of the Deccan or in a brand-new factory site.

The tourist industry is also developing fast. The country's almost unlimited potentialities are still far from exhausted, but groups of tourists organized by the international agencies are already flocking to visit India's most famous sights and anyone who is not afraid to travel alone will not lack for advice, transport and accommodation on his way to see the treasures of Indian culture illustrated in this book and countless others besides. Moreover, in encouraging tourism among foreign visitors, the Indians have discovered the attractions that travel in their own country can provide, and this to an extent that pride in the monuments of its glorious past has in part taken the place of incitement to religious pilgrimage. The old temple-cities and caves, however remote from the main lines of communication, the Buddhist monuments and the Muslim mosques and tombs, which until fairly recently were deserted, are swarming with visitors now, especially on holidays; schoolchildren are taken on conducted tours, and, if belief in the holiness of these places has dwindled, it has been replaced by pride in the nation's history and achievements.

Dazzled by the magnificent heritage of ancient kings and sages and the spectacular achievements of the modern age in the cities and industrial concerns, the visitor tends to overlook India 'proper', the India of the villages, in which the country's destiny is still being—and will continue for a long time to be—shaped. Of all the experiments undertaken by the reformers, none has been of such vital importance as the 'Community Projects', which aim to free the village community from the ancient bonds of the caste-system and from outmoded methods of cultivation; to create for the peasant a new, free society and to teach him to make better use of his native soil. In Shamaspur, near Delhi, I visited one of the villages, which is a model for the 600,000 throughout India. I propose to complete the series of pictures in this book with a photograph of the chairman of its local council; he is a Harijan, until recently an Untouchable; his face shows pride and a sense of responsibility but also something of the immense underlying melancholy of this country, the tragedy of a social system thousands of years old, based upon inequality before god and man.

NOTES TO THE PLATES

319 New Delhi. Rashtrapati Bhawan, residence of the president of the republic, designed by Sir Edward Lutyens and built as the viceroy's palace in red and white sandstone with copper-covered dome

320 New Delhi. Mounting of the guard at the President's Palace

321 New Delhi. The Lakshmi-Narayan Temple, founded by Jugal Kishore Birla and opened in 1939

322 Madras. Armenian church from the early 18th century

323 Calcutta. The Roman Catholic Cathedral of St Maria of the Rose-Garland in the Barabazar quarter, built in 1797

324 Pondicherry (Puducheri). View from the pier of the centre of the city, which was founded by François Martin in 1674, with the towers of the Church of Notre Dame des Anges, built in 1855

325 Calcutta. The 'Scotch Kirk' of St Andrews, 1818

326 Delhi. Circuit House, now part of the University to the north of the city, formerly the residence of the viceroy before his palace was built in New Delhi

327 Calcutta. The Victoria Memorial, a museum built in white marble at the instigation of Lord Curzon; architect Sir William Emerson, opened in 1921

328 Patna. The post office with the façade in classical style, characteristic of the colonial period

329 Bombay. Victorian public building of the late 19th century

330 Bombay. On the Apollo Bunder, where formerly the passenger-steamers were moored, the Gateway of India was erected in yellow basalt to commemorate George V's landing there in December 1911

331 Bombay. A typical 19th century street in the Indian residential and business quarter

332 Bombay. Marine Drive, the promenade along Back Bay with its impressive front of modern buildings

333 New Delhi. The two blocks of the Secretariat were designed by Sir Herbert Baker and completed in 1930; they stand on one side of the square on Raisina Hill in front of the Presidential Palace and together they form the 'Acropolis' of the new city

334 New Delhi. The main entrance of the circular Parliament building, which was opened in January 1927; architect Sir Herbert Baker

335 Bangalore. Vidhan Soudha, the palace built for the State of Mysore in which the parliament and government offices are housed

336 Bombay. The government building of Maharashtra State (Bombay State until 1960), built in the 'fifties

337 Chandigarh. The Palace of Justice, the first to be completed of the state buildings planned by Le Corbusier

338 Chandigarh. The Secretariat, a government building in reinforced concrete designed by Le Corbusier

339 Ahmedabad. Modern municipal building (Municipal Major Dairy)

340 Ahmedabad. The Museum, built to the design of Le Corbusier

341 Ahmedabad. The Milkowners' Association building, built by Le Corbusier

342 Chandigarh. Junior Secondary School; architect, Pierre Jeanneret

343 Jamma Scheme canal, Kalsi. (Photo by R. R. Bharadwaj, Bombay)

344 At Jamshedpur one of India's major industrial centres grew up around the Tata Steelworks. (Photo by R. R. Bharadwaj, Bombay)

345 West Bengal. Scene in one of the jute factories near Calcutta. (Photo by R. R. Bharadwaj, Bombay)

346–352 Indian types:

346 A member of one of the primitive tribes from the jungle areas: Kadu from the West Ghats of Mysore province

347 Young girl from Orissa

348 Brahman, Tamil, with the Vishnu sign on his forehead, at Kanchipuram

349 Young man from Assam

350 A Bengali college professor from Calcutta

351 Rajput from Udaipur

352 Village headman, formerly an 'untouchable' (Harijan), near Delhi

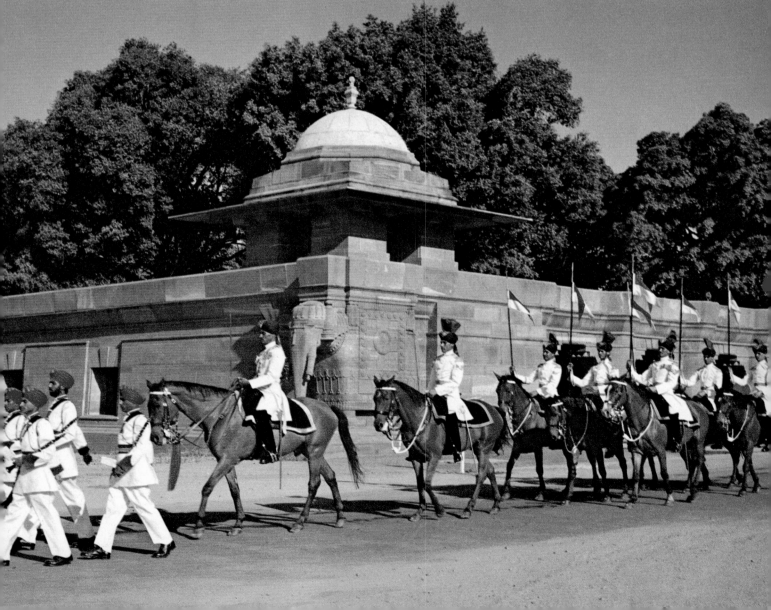

322 MADRAS

323 CALCUTTA

324 PONDICHE[RY]

325 CALCUTTA

327 CALCUTTA

328 PATNA

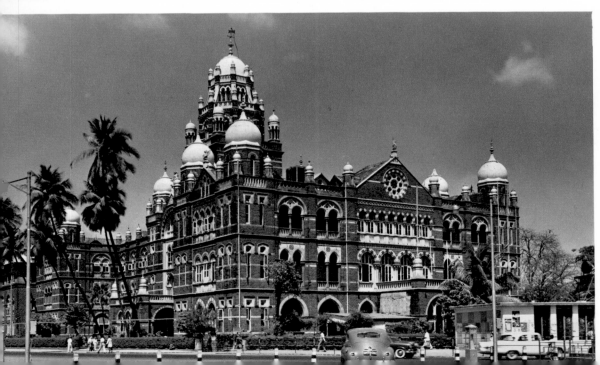

329 BOMBAY

330 BOMBAY,
GATEWAY OF INDIA

331 BOMBAY

332 BOMBAY,
MARINE DRIVE

333 NEW DELHI, SECRETARIAT

334 NEW DELHI, PARLIAMENT

335 BANGALORE

336 BOMBAY

337-338 CHANDIGARH

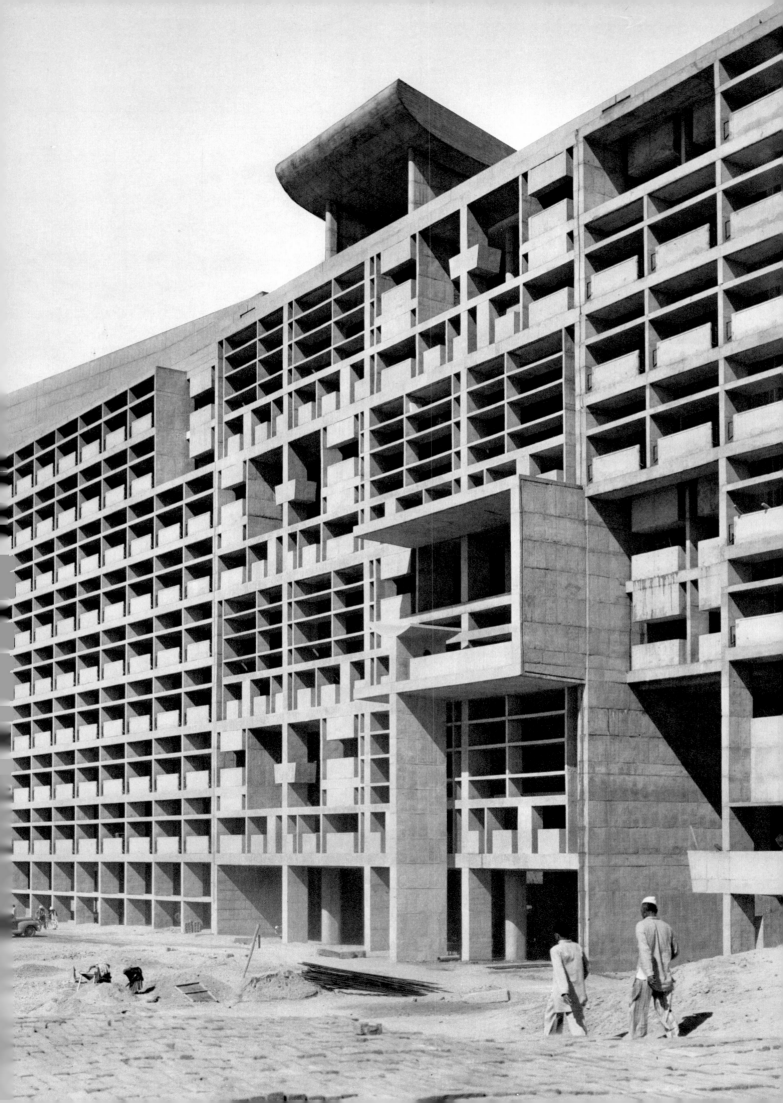

339-340 AHMEDABAD

340

AHMEDABAD

CHANDIGARH

343 JAMNA SCHEME, KALSI

344 TATA STEEL WORKS, JAMSHEDPUR
345 JUTE MILLS, WEST BENGAL

346
347

348

349

350

351

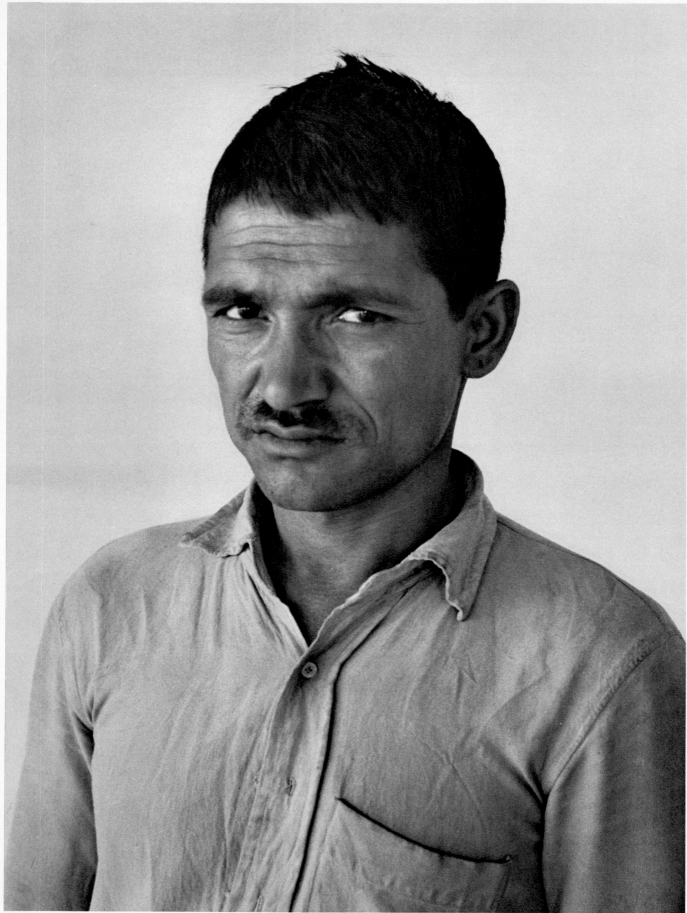

INDEX OF PLATES

The author would like to thank all those persons and organizations whose advice and help he found invaluable in organizing his travels and obtaining his photographs, more particularly the representatives of the Indian Tourist Office as well as of Air India and Swissair.

The prints for illustrations 313 (Photograph by Heinz-Friedel Vogenbeck), 317 (Photograph by Hedda Morrison) and 318 (Photograph by Kulwant Roy) were obtained from the Atlantis-Archiv. The prints for illustrations 343–345 were provided by R. R. Bharadwaj, Bombay. All other photographs were taken by the author during his travels in 1926–28 and 1958–65.

Names have been spelt in accordance with official English usage in India.

The maps were drawn by Arthur Dürst.